# The Venison Cookbook
## for Beginners

Cheri Helregel

Published by

 **krause publications**

700 E. State Street • Iola, WI 54990-0001
Telephone: 715/445-2214

Please call or write for our free catalog of outdoor publications.
Our toll-free number to place an order or obtain a free catalog is 800-258-0929
or please use our regular business telephone 715-445-2214
for editorial comment and further information.

Library of Congress Catalog Number: 98-87367
ISBN: 0-87341-693-7
Printed in the United States of America

Check out our Web site at www.ohdeer.com

*This book is humbly dedicated to the One who gave His life for me, Jesus Christ, and to the three most precious people in my life:*

*my husband, Mark,*
*and*
*my daughters, Nicole and Natalie.*

# Acknowledgments

Special thanks to my husband, Mark, who provided much-needed encouragement throughout this entire project. Thanks, too, for supporting my desire to work at home. Your sacrifices made this project possible. It is such a joy and honor to be able to serve my family.

Thank you, Nicole, for all your encouragement and your sweet, sweet prayers. God listened and answered! Thank you, Natalie, for showing me how to be joyful even when times are tough. You really are a trooper! I love you both!

To my Mom, Aunt Lyda and Daphne. Thanks for supporting me in my walk with Christ. Thanks for always pointing me back to Him when things were looking grim. Thanks for having faith in Christ and for having faith that He would complete the work in me that He started.

Many, many thanks to my husband's family, Dick, Kay and Janice. For without your wisdom, advice and encouragement, we might never have bothered to embrace venison as a daily blessing for our family. Thanks for getting me started with those first few recipes. Thanks too, for your love!

To all my friends in Christ, particularly Lori, Michelle, Donna and Carmen. Your friendship, prayers, encouragement and support mean so much. Thank you!!

To Mark Hartrich and Hartrich Meats, Inc., for your years of service and for sharing your knowledge.

To Noel Laurent. For your faith and dedication to serving Christ through the *Illinois Sportsmen Against Hunger* program and for all your help with this project.

To the folks at Krause Publications,

Don, for taking my first call. Paul, for giving me a chance and for answering my endless list of questions. Kevin, for making me look like a better writer than I am by loaning your talented gifts to this project. I have enjoyed the privilege of working with and learning from you.

To my Heavenly Father, who has faithfully provided all that we need. Who gave me the inspiration and desire to write this book. Who graciously provided me with the strength and knowledge necessary to complete it. Whom I love, because You first loved me.

*"Commit everything you do to the Lord. Trust Him, and He will help you."*
Psalm 37:5 (NLT)

# Table of Contents

# Introduction

## Beyond Sausage and Jerky...Why I Wrote This Book

I married a wonderful, brilliant, highly intelligent man who enjoys dressing in camouflage, roaming through the woods, braving cold, wet elements of early winter to sit in a tree for several hours until his rump goes numb, just so he can hunt and kill deer. He is a hunter.

The first time my husband excitedly called to announce he had killed a deer, the following thoughts rushed through my head…. "Well how wonderful…but…oh, dear! What in the world are we going to do with a deer?!! Can I really eat Bambi? What will it taste like and how do I cook it? Do we really HAVE to eat it?"

After all, perhaps this particular deer had a different calling in life than to end up in my freezer. If you are the spouse of a hunter, perhaps you've pondered these very same questions.

Though many hunters aren't terribly picky about how they eat their venison, the rest of us usually need to overcome various emotional, mental and physical challenges in order to enjoy a tasty deer dining experience. In my desperate attempts to consume an entire deep freeze full of professionally butchered venison before the next hunting season, I began a search and consulted what few resources were available for preparing and cooking venison.

In my quest, I queried various seasoned hunters to discover how they preferred to eat their venison. Most of them suggested dashing a little salt and pepper on venison and then tossing it on the grill. Soaking steaks in Italian salad dressing was the second runner up to good ol' salt and pepper. Though these cooking methods suited them just fine, I quickly decided that their well-intended advice did not produce our desired palatal results. I was also quite amazed to discover that many hunters I questioned process their venison into 80+ pounds of sausage and jerky. I could have collected dozens of recipes for summer sausage and jerky, but I just knew there had to be a better, more productive way to utilize our young buck that sacrificed his life to nourish our bodies.

My thoughtful, attentive husband, trying his best to offer suggestions, would pass along recipes from his "outdoor, woodsy, huntsman" magazines or order recipe books published by the same "outdoor, woodsy" hunters. I often found many of these recipes to be either impractical or used varying degrees of salt, pepper and more of the same. I was amused to find that a good many of these recipes were intended for the hunter who prefers cooking out in the wilderness, listing such ingredients as twine, twigs, wild berries, wild herb rubs or worse! Thanks, but no thanks! While there is no doubt in my mind this type of cooking requires an enormous amount of talent and skill, I prefer to remain in the kitchen to cook my game.

I eventually stumbled across some fancy wild game cookbooks at a large bookstore only to discover that they offered extremely gourmet recipes that required highly impractical ingredients and cooking methods. Though these recipes sounded very tasty, since I was a working mother at the time, I did not have two weeks to shop in specialty stores looking for odd, expensive ingredients; two weeks to learn how to use my new kitchen accessories; and two hours to prepare my cuisine. However, one of these days I would like to share them with a friend of mine who enjoys gourmet cooking and invite myself to dinner. (Ahem! Are you listening, George?)

Finally, after several years of experimenting in the kitchen, working from and building upon a few basic recipes and some very helpful hints from my mother-in-law, I have finally developed or converted many delicious and practical recipes for cooking venison. And I love it! When folks find out that our diet consists primarily of venison, they suddenly become intrigued and curious, especially about the delicious entree they just ate. Eventually, I found myself describing how to cook venison and touting its benefits so often I decided to write "Oh Deer! The Venison Cookbook for Beginners," so that I could share my trials, tribulations, successes and resultant blessings with those who have vowed to love, honor and cherish their hunter or even for those veteran hunters who want to go beyond sausage and jerky.

# Compelling Reasons to Reconsider Venison

Are you a little squeamish at the thought of handling, preparing or cooking venison? If so, you are not alone. I am sure hundreds, perhaps even thousands have wrinkled their noses at the very notion of feasting on venison. In fact, it's a fairly common response among those who hear for the first time that my family frequently dines on venison. However, as I proceed to explain several compelling reasons to reconsider venison as a quality meat source for a healthy diet, their hesitant attitude quickly becomes an optimistic "hmm…maybe." If you have difficulty motivating yourself to serve venison at the dinner table, consider the following:

## Reason # 1 – Nutritional profiles of Vinny Venison and Benny Beef

I would like to introduce you to Vinny Venison. As you can see by his muscle tone, he is very athletic and svelte. Thanks to his highly aerobic daily routine of running through the woods he only has about 10% body fat. Always glowing with energy, you can usually find Vinny munching on whole grains, leafy greens or drinking lots of fresh water. His all-natural diet and lifestyle has done a lot to keep him fit and healthy.

I would also like for you to meet Benny Beef. After a slow walk across the pasture, Benny looks noticeably tired and sweaty. His steroid-enriched diet has contributed to recent excessive and rapid weight gain. Benny carries about 30-40% body fat. Constantly fighting infections, Benny also takes a maintenance antibiotic preparation.

| 3.5 ounce serving | Calories | Fat | Protein | Cholesterol |
|---|---|---|---|---|
| Venison | 149 | 1.4g | 23.6g | 116mg |
| 75 % Lean Ground Beef | 260 | 19g | 27g | 100mg |

Above all other reasons, nutrition is the most compelling reason to reconsider venison as a quality red meat source for your family's diet. Ounce per ounce, venison is significantly lower in fat and calories than beef, yet provides more protein. You get almost all of the nutritional benefits of red meat with 80-85 percent less fat.

Also, assuming your deer was hunted and not commercially raised, you can be fairly sure that your venison will be free of steroids and antibiotics. Commercial beef producers frequently use steroids to increase meat production or growth. They also administer antibiotics to prevent infections…some of which are caused by complications of steroid use! Your average whitetail deer dines on grain, grass, shrubs and other vegetarian delights that are full of nature's finest fiber, soy protein and minerals. We all should eat so well. But since most of us don't enjoy grazing on clover, nibbling whole grains or munching tree leaves, we can benefit from the deer's healthy eating habits by putting venison on the dinner table.

## Reason # 2 - Eat a little venison, save a load of money!!

Okay, so let's assume that whether or not you start cooking venison, your hunter is a true predator and will spare no dime in funding his or her hobby. In other words, if we exclude the investment (sacrifice?) in high-tech hunting gear and only consider what it costs to purchase a hunting license and process your venison, you can reduce your grocery bill by hundreds of dollars each year. Have you thought about what you could do with hundreds of dollars? If the Lord has blessed you with a hunter, making good use of your venison is one more way you can be a good steward of the money and resources God has given you. Sit and think a minute about how you would choose to spend nearly $200.

We have our venison commercially processed and add 20% pork (80% lean) to our ground venison. With that in mind, we end up with about

70 pounds of venison from one deer that costs a total of $80. That averages out to $1.14 per pound, *for all cuts of meat.* The tenderloins, the round steaks, the cube steaks, the roasts and the ground meat all cost $1.14 per pound. One average-sized deer lasts our family of two adults and two children about six months. Two average-sized processed deer would last us all year.

Depending on the type and quality of beef you purchase, you could spend anywhere from $1.39 to $1.99 or more per pound. To get 140 pounds of beef at $1.99 per pound, you would spend $278.60. And remember, $1.99 per pound means you won't be buying a lot of prime cuts from the butcher. If you were to buy good-quality steaks and roasts (like the ones you get when your deer is processed professionally) you could easily spend nearly twice that. For the sake of argument, I'll assume you are a wise shopper and can get away with spending only $300 per year to buy an equal amount of beef.

You do the math…$300 (beef) minus $160 (venison) comes to $140. Now, what did you decide you could do with that extra money?

My husband normally hunts in the fall, so we end up getting our commercially processed venison near the end of December or the first week of January. Just imagine having the majority of your red meat paid off in one month and feasting on it for the rest of the year! Picture yourself going to the grocery store and not buying expensive meat all the time! How much less would your grocery bill be sans meat? Since I also buy my poultry in bulk at a club warehouse, I rarely ever buy meat when I go grocery store. Remember that extra cash? Since you'll be spending less time and money at the supermarket, you'll have more time to think about where to spend or stash your extra cash.

## Reason # 3 - Gotta Make Room for Ben and Jerry's

When my husband hauled home those first little white packages marked "Wild Game - Not for Sale", I had not yet overcome my objections to cooking and eating venison. In determining what to do with the 80 pounds of frozen meat, I considered all my options and came up with what I thought was a fabulous solution. We had a modest-size freezer in the garage with lots of room to spare, so I figured I would just stow it away under the Ben and Jerry's ice cream. Out of sight, out of mind, right? Well, that only worked until the next hunting season rolled around. I either had to start cooking venison or purchase another freezer to hold the next kill. There was also one other problem I had overlooked: With the freezer full of venison, there was no room for any more Ben and Jerry's ice cream. I started cooking venison because we needed the room. I mean, that ice cream would start to melt soon, we *needed* the room.

Are you one of those folks who has more venison than you know what to do with, because you didn't know what to do with it? I empathize and I urge you to begin cooking today. Start with the Zesty Chili recipe (page 102). It is probably the easiest recipe to fix and I assure you it is tasty. I always get rave reviews on this dish – even from folks who don't know there's venison in the pot. By the way, what have you got to lose if it doesn't turn out? A failed venison recipe is just a stepping stone to future success. Besides, you can always whip up a grilled cheese or egg sandwich at the last minute to save the day.

If you're concerned that you still have too much venison stored up, load some grocery bags with various cuts and give them to your friends along with a copy of this book. After a few weeks, you'll all be swapping new recipes, cooking tips and techniques. Please be sure to share them with me, hmmm? (see page 151)

If you find yourself overwhelmed with an abundance of venison in your freezer as the hunting season approaches, consider donating your next deer kill to local food pantries through participating sporting organizations and meat processors. For more information on how to donate your deer kill to food pantries in your area, read Chapter 8, *Hunters for the Hungry.* This chapter also includes a list of agencies and phone numbers for each state and for Canada.

## Reason # 4 - Because you love him…(or her, as the case may be)

For those of you who are reading this book and happen to be the 'spouse of a hunter,' you may already do several things, on a daily basis, out of love for your hunter. You're likely cooking meals, giving them attention, washing smelly hunting gear (whew! what is that stuff anyways?), etc. So why not make your hunter feel even more loved and appreciated by cooking the venison that's brought home. We all know most hunters hunt because it's a hobby or calling in life, and not always the sole means of putting a meal on the table. Cooking the venison makes hunting even more of a family affair, providing an extra sense of pride and togetherness. This positive reinforcement is essential in helping to build a healthy and stable family. It also encourages hunters to continue hunting year after year, thus allowing you to continue enjoying your own hunting (aka: shopping…perhaps) trips.

Seriously though, by making productive use of the resources our hunters' have provided, we are also honoring God for the true blessings that our hunters and their gifts are to us.

# What Can I Expect?

So there you stand in the kitchen, with a little white package of meat staring you in the face. You are mortified at what you might find underneath the wrapper because the only printing on the package boldly proclaims in bright red letters "WILD GAME – NOT FOR SALE!". Wild game? You begin to wonder, "Hmmmm, just exactly what does that mean? Is it aggressive? Will it jump out and attack me as soon as I tear off the tape?" You brace yourself for the worst and, as the fear rises from the pit of your stomach, you start bludgeoning the package with a meat tenderizer then wrestle it into the trash compactor and congratulate yourself for narrowly escaping such a traumatic encounter.

Now folks, hopefully the previous scenario does not describe you, but if it does, just take a deep breath, relax and read on as I describe what you can expect to see, feel, smell and taste as you work with venison. It's not that bad…really…honest…trust me.

The often-intimidating term "wild game" that is stamped on your package simply means the meat has been hunted by an individual (your hubby, perhaps?) and not produced and raised on a meat farm. The meat processor, by law, is required to stamp all processed wild game with this statement, along with the decree, "not for sale." Some folks are inclined to believe this means the meat is not suitable for human consumption. Fortunately, this term implies nothing of the sort.

Market hunting, hunting animals to be sold as food, was made illegal in the United States right around 1900. These laws were enacted to protect game animals from over-hunting and possible extinction. There are, however, various deer ranches that import, breed and raise European, Australian and Oriental deer specifically for trade. Yep, that's right....folks actually BUY foreign-bred venison to eat so they can prepare a fancy gourmet dish to impress their dinner guests. If you are interested in trying some of this "farm-raised" venison, refer to the appendix for more information.

## What color is your "red" meat, and why?

Did you know that not all red meat is actually red? Most of what you see as bright "red" in the meat section at your grocery store is caused by a preservative added to the meat to enrich the color (and supposedly retain freshness). Although venison is considered a "red" meat, depending upon the cut, its color can actually appear to be a deeper, darker red, almost purple or plum colored.

"Purple!", you exclaim. "You expect me to eat PURPLE meat?!"

Well, sure. Why not? What kind of apples do you eat? Red, yellow, green or all three? Do you eat apples, regardless of their color? Some apples taste better straight from the tree while others taste better in pies, cookies or sauce. While deer do not grow on trees (overpopulation in some areas, might make it seem that way), I've compared venison to apples in order to help you better understand its purpose and flexibility in a red-meat diet. You'll find that venison and beef are different. Venison is not bad, foul or scary, it's just *different*. My goal is to help you identify these differences and help you appreciate each unique difference and how it can appeal to your sensory preferences.

## A smell is worth a thousand words...

In my early years of becoming acquainted with venison in the kitchen, I found myself troubled by the *odd* (ie: different) smell that wafted above the skillet as I experimented with various recipes. My husband noted that while everyone else at the table gobbled up what I had just cooked, I sat there a little green in the face not able to bring the fork to my mouth. I could not differentiate between what I had smelled the entire time I was cooking (reminder: different, not necessarily *bad*) and what I might taste. Since then, I discovered that by adding various simple yet familiar ingredients (like onion, celery, and garlic) to my recipes, it greatly enhanced the flavor of venison and rescued my sense of smell. With these additions I didn't become overly focused on the simmering venison alone. I also found the crock pot to be an extremely valuable wild game cooking tool. Since the crock pot does most of the cooking, I found it wasn't necessary to slave over the stove to properly cook the meat. It also allowed me to remove the "new smells" from my aromatic memory before I served the dish.

After a few short weeks of using these simple cooking methods, I found myself learning to appreciate the aroma of simmering venison, anticipating the moment that I could eat the delicious, satisfying and healthy meal. Funny too, how after several years of cooking primarily venison for our family, every once in awhile when I cook with beef, I now find the smell of simmering beef to be odd or different – but not foul or bad…just different. Funny how we so quickly become creatures of habit.

## So, what does it taste like?

If you are pondering the question, "So, what does venison really taste like?" chances are you haven't actually tasted venison, not knowingly anyway. It's actually very difficult to explain what venison tastes like…and that's not because the taste is bad since venison is such a versatile meat to cook with, to actually explain the taste depends upon how it has been cooked and what it is cooked with. Venison, literally, complements your recipes.

To explain further, let me begin with our old buddy, beef, again. Do you know what gives beef the strong flavor that we normally associate with beef? It's not a pretty word (or sight), but it is primarily the *fat* in beef that gives beef such a strong, robust flavor. This juicy flavor is also why we often prefer to leave fat on beef, despite repeated health warnings to trim the fat. Ironically, since we refer to venison as wild game, people just assume that the meat will have a strong flavor. Guess what! I've got good news! It's not as strong as you would think, or at least it shouldn't be. This, of course, assumes you are cooking with venison that came from a properly processed, averaged-sized deer. Since venison has far less fat that beef, the intensity of the taste is far less than that of beef. You might be thinking "Yeah, so what does that mean?" What that means is venison has a greater potential to complement your recipes, whereas beef has the potential to dominate your recipes.

For example, when you cook chili, do you add beef because you want your chili to taste like beef? Of course not! You just want a little meat in your chili so that it will complement the basic flavors provided by the tomatoes, peppers and spices. Venison, because of its low fat content and mild flavor, does a great job of absorbing the chili spices and flavors thus complementing the chili very well. Often there is the misconception that we add venison to chili to "mask the wild flavor of the meat." That's not the case at all. Venison simply makes the chili taste better! Also, since there is little or no gristle in ground venison, it simmers, browns and crumbles into a very fine meat mixture which, I believe, adds a unique, appealing texture to many common dinner recipes.

There is one last thing I must mention about venison. Much like any other red meat, the younger the meat, the more tender it will be and the better it will taste. Most of the tastes and smells I described above are assuming that your venison is from a young to average-age deer (not a big old buck). I also assume that proper care, field dressing and aging processes were used after killing the deer. Older and larger bucks will have a stronger taste and a tougher texture, so more care will need to be taken to remove any and all fat. Although older buck meat is edible and can be used with most of the cooking methods and recipes I've described in this book, I firmly believe that big old bucks belong mounted on the wall and turned into sausage, not stored in your freezer. Do yourself a favor and convince your hunter to kill a young deer for the freezer and pursue the BIG ones for the wall only.

# Key Ingredients For a Successful Venison Recipe

One of my goals in writing this book is to provide enough information that you, the reader, will feel empowered to modify, identify and create scrumptious venison recipes. Hopefully after fixing a few of the recipes I've included in the book, you'll have several successful experiences under your apron and the courage to step out, vary a little, and perhaps write your own book. That's how I did it.

There are various sauces, liquids, spices and dry ingredients that, in differing combinations, contribute to create a successful venison recipe.

## Sauces/Liquids

Here is a list of some sauces and liquids that will help your venison recipes. Those marked with a (T) act as a tenderizing agent for the tougher cuts while others are a quick and powerful way to add flavor. Some only add moisture and flavor to the meat or recipe. You can pick and choose the ones you think you might like. Some of my favorites are:

    barbecue or Sloppy Joe sauce
    broth, beef or chicken
    catsup
    chili sauce
    cooking wines
    cranberry and other fruit sauces
    French onion soup, condensed (T)
    gravy, canned
    honey
    hot pepper sauce
    lemon juice (T)
    mustard (T)
    soy sauce (T)
    taco sauce
    Teriyaki sauce (T)
    tomato sauce/juice/puree (T)
    tomato soup, condensed
    tomatoes, stewed/diced (canned) (T)
    vinegar (T)
    Worcestershire Sauce (T)

## Spices/Dry Ingredients

These flavor-enhancers are very versatile and interchangeable. Some of the fresh varieties also add moisture. Some of my favorites include:
black pepper
    bouillon cubes, beef or chicken
    brown sugar
    celery, coarsely or finely chopped
    celery salt or celery seed
    cilantro, dried or fresh

chili powder
cumin, ground
dry soup mixes (onion, etc)
garlic, minced or pureed
garlic salt or powder
green pepper, chopped
Italian seasoning
onion, coarsely or finely chopped
onion salt and powder
oregano
paprika
parsley, dried or fresh

## Additional Fat/Moisture Sources

Since venison is so low in fat, additional fat sources add flavor and moisture to enhance various recipes. Typically, there are usually only one or two fat sources (if any) per recipe. They are not easily interchangeable. Good ones include:

bacon
broth, beef or chicken
butter (sparingly)
Campbell's Golden Mushroom Soup
cheese
cooking oil (sparingly)
cream of chicken or cream of mushroom soup
eggs
milk
sour cream
water

# How To Spot A Good Recipe For Venison Substitution

After you have cooked a few recipes from this book and experienced for yourself how venison graciously responds to the flavors of various spices, sauces and flavorings, start looking for potential recipes for venison substitution. Your personal experiences combined with the Three Key Ingredients Lists should help you identify, modify and create a tasty new venison recipe.

When I'm on the lookout for a potential new venison recipe, I first target recipes that include beef or pork (and chicken too!). Then I look to see if it includes any ingredients that will aid in tenderizing a tougher cut of meat or if I can adapt it to the crock pot way of life (which is very important for me). I'll often find that I need to add or incorporate a little onion and/or celery into any new recipe I try. This is, however, my personal preference. I may also find that I need to remove an ingredient that I know does not work as well with venison and substitute something that works better. I also look for opportunities to incorporate ground venison into a recipe that calls for a cut of meat that is not ground. For example, one day I decided to try out our Venison Steak Marinade recipe on hamburgers and it was a big hit!

## There's No Place Like Home…For A Home-Cooked Meal

One of the best places to start looking for new venison recipes is right in your very own kitchen….perhaps in a tattered wooden box with the word "RECIPES" still barely inscribed on the front. For your first effort, go easy on yourself and try not to make it too complicated. In other words, pass over the temptation to select a challenging recipe like Spinach Stuffed Filet Mignons with au jus. Pick something that is simple. Perhaps a traditional family spaghetti or chili recipe. Better yet, find a recipe that may not even require you to make any adjustments, because they already have a few Key Ingredients for a Successful Venison Recipe. For example, when confronted with the dilemma of making wise use of a venison arm roast (HUGE, HUGE hunk of roast), I poured through countless cookbooks searching for good pot roast recipe that would inspire within me a meal suitable and pleasing to even God Himself. Not having much luck, I set aside my grand illusions and went back to my recipe box, where I rediscovered a very simple, yet tasty recipe for Italian Beef. Furthermore, much as I tried to find something to fudge, fiddle with or otherwise change, it appeared that my venison arm roast would make a fine pot of Italian Roast Sandwiches (p. 124) without tampering one bit with the original concept. Lo and behold, it did, and boy was it a huge hit with my husband. And to think I almost abused that huge hunk of meat by turning it into a pot roast. Too bad there are only two arm roasts per deer.

You may have already guessed that Italian- and Mexican-based recipes are often some of the easiest recipes to convert to venison. At least that has been my personal experience. By their very nature, Italian and Mexican dishes include an abundance of strong, aromatic spices that are easily absorbed by venison (especially ground meat) during the cooking process. These spices enhance the overall flavor of your recipe.

Now, back to spaghetti. I've selected spaghetti as a practical example of how easy it is to begin to incorporate venison into your normal meal planning. Our family loves spaghetti. As a mom, I personally love spaghetti. But, not so much for the flavor appeal. After an exhausting and stressful day at work, I can usually whip up spaghetti and have it on the table in less than 30 minutes, even if the ground meat is frozen to the core because I just couldn't the find the time to plan the day's dinner meal in between picking the peanut butter out of my daughter's hair and discovering my gas tank was on empty just as I headed out 15 minutes late for work! Get the picture? Refer to the next chapter on quick defrosting tips.

Dinner ala spaghetti for this *Enjoli* woman (I can bring home the bacon…da da da dum, fry it up in a pan…da da da dum…remember that?) was to throw the spaghetti in a pot of boiling water, dump a jar of CLASSICO's finest in a saucepan and fry up some meat to add to the spaghetti sauce. While that was all boiling and simmering away, I popped a few pieces of Butternut in the toaster. The golden-brown bread was later bathed in margarine laced with garlic powder…walah! Garlic toast! Ideally, this meal all came together in a timely fashion as I served it with a smile to my adoring family who had so graciously set the table for me while I slaved over their internationally inspired meal. And if you believe that, I have a deer to sell you that has three arm roasts.

For most folks, life is a constant merry-go-round. How in the world can we ever find time to experiment with venison and new recipes? Well, the good news is that you don't have to find the time, it's already there. All we have to do is incorporate venison into our normal (is there such a thing?), everyday lifestyle. Don't necessarily change your lifestyle for the sake of the venison. Make venison work for you, not the other way around. In order to overcome my early objections to the new, unfamiliar aroma of simmering venison, I simply added a little chopped celery, onion and garlic. My nose appreciates this blend of spices and aromas and proceeds to tell my stomach it's time to eat. What resulted was a very tasty and satisfying spaghetti dish that we all heartily devoured. Believe it or not, my family actually prefers ground venison over ground beef in these types of dishes…because the venison recipes are so much more flavorful.

## Hazardous Taste Warning

There is one notable exception to the practical suggestion of starting simple. Beware of various commercially prepared seasonings and mixes such as Hamburger Helper and pre-packaged taco seasoning. After attempting to incorporate some ground venison into one of those Hamburger Helper mixes, it didn't take long for me to realize that unlike what the packaging suggests, it did not help the hamburger. Instead, because the fat and flavor of hamburger is so pleasantly strong, the hamburger literally saves the mix. I, unfortunately, discovered that my lean venison eagerly absorbed the harsh, pungent dehydrated spices along with the exorbitantly salty preservatives and MSG. I wouldn't feed it to a dog, much less my family.

Likewise for my attempts to use a taco seasoning mix with ground venison. The first time I attempted to make tacos with venison, using a packaged taco seasoning mix, I resolved myself to the fact that tacos and venison did not make a meal fit for human consumption. As I stared at the radiant orange-colored slop sitting on the table along side a wonderful spread of accompaniments such as tomatoes, lettuce, cheese, sour cream, etc., I began to wonder, "Just what's in that mix that makes the meat glow so brightly colored orange?" As an ill feeling crept up on me, I figured it was just as well that I didn't know. Again, I discovered that the robust flavor of beef barely saved the taco seasoning mix. The mix certainly did not add any enhancements to the beef.

However, being the taco-loving family that we are (speaking on behalf of my 7-year-old daughter), I had to find a way to use venison in tacos. Otherwise, what kind of reject Mom would I be anyway? You may be wondering, "Are good venison tacos possible?" Well, yes actually, and it's quite simple. One day while browning some ground venison, onions, celery and garlic for chili, I wondered what it would taste like if I added some hot sauce to the equation…Walah! I had a wonderful, robust and naturally flavored taco meat that wasn't neon orange!! My family thinks these tacos are so wonderful that we named them *The Best Tacos in Town*. My 7-year-old daughter said they were even better than you-know-who's tacos. It just doesn't get any better than that, now does it? And, what's really cool is that *The Best Tacos in Town* are super-duper low in fat. We won't mention how many fat grams are in a taco from you-know-who, just in case you ate one or two or three or four (maybe more) today. I wouldn't want you to get depressed.

## Mid-Life Cooking Crisis

Now, once you've figured out how easy it is to incorporate venison into your normal, everyday cooking, you may find yourself wanting to explore recipes beyond that of your tried-and-true recipe box. "Why?" you might ask, "would I want to forsake my family recipes to try something new?" This is exactly what I said when my husband shoved a book in my hand that had enough chili recipes in it to feed a Third World country. I happened to adore my traditional family chili recipe and so did he, or so I thought. For years he gobbled up my chili without ever indicating he wanted something different. Oh, I guess he eventually made a few comments about not wanting tomato chunks in the chili anymore, but I thought it was just a bad football day and didn't think anymore of it. Turns out, he was just tired of the same old, same old. Mid-life crisis, you wonder? Maybe so, but at least he didn't want a different wife, just a different chili recipe. On a totally side note, "Hmmm, I wonder if I should change my hair style?"

With this in mind, I set out to find another fantastic chili recipe. This turned out to be some of the best advice my husband ever gave me. Not only did it save me from my venison cooking rut, but it eventually led to my writing this book. Plus, my *Zesty Chili* recipe is one of the most raved-about dishes I cart off to potluck and social functions. However, in searching for an alternative chili recipe, most of the venison chili recipes I found made enough chili to feed our entire village of 1,800 people. For some reason, when folks cook with venison, they tend to do it in large portions. I'm not sure yet why this is so. Perhaps they are in such a hurry to get rid of their venison because they don't quite know how cook it. What usually happens is those who don't know how to cook venison will shove it off on some poor unsuspecting soul who has never eaten venison. That person then walks away with such a negative experience that they vow never to eat venison again. If you happen to be one of those people, I hope after reading this book you have the grace to forgive that person and the courage to give venison another chance at satisfying your cautious taste buds.

So, how did I manage to concoct another chili recipe? Well, I perused and selected a few recipes with ingredients that appeared to meet my husband's criteria for a 'better chili'. Then, I taped them all to the garage wall and threw darts at them to decide which ingredients I should use in what quantities. Well, okay, not really. I know it sounds a little intimidating, but seriously, I just did a little nip and tuck on each recipe and incorporated a few of my own tried-and-true cooking techniques. If this still sounds kind of scary to you, in the next section I'll do a play-by-play translation of a recipe I found and how I adapted it to venison.

## Venison, Pearls and Lace

One day I was perusing my limited collection of fancy cookbooks in search of a dish worthy to grace itself at a romantic dinner for two. I came across a recipe for Burgundy Beef Stroganoff. This was one of those recipes that appealed to my sense of sight because the picture included in the cookbook looked absolutely exquisite! Noting that it already listed several key ingredients for a successful venison substitution, I pulled out my trusty pencil and started nipping, tucking and whittling away. Here's an illustration of how I fine-tuned that noble recipe:

## Burgundy Beef Stroganoff

2 pounds round steak, cut into ¼-inch strips  *use less meat*
2 tablespoons margarine
4 medium onions, sliced (about 3 cups)  *use less onion*
1/4 cup all-purpose flour  *more*
1 cup beef broth  *increase liquid*
1/2 cup burgundy or other dry red wine
3 tablespoons tomato paste
1/2 teaspoon ground thyme
3/4 cup sour cream  *add garlic + celery while venison*
Hot buttered noodles  *is browning*

In large skillet, over medium heat, brown meat in margarine. Stir in onions and cook for 3 minutes; remove from heat. Sprinkle flour over meat and stir until well combined. Stir in beef broth, wine, tomato paste and thyme until smooth. Cook and stir over medium heat until sauce is thickened and begins to boil. Cover; cook over low heat for 40 to 45 minutes or until tender. Stir sour cream into sauce. (Do not boil). Serve over hot buttered noodles.

*put in crockpot add sour cream just before serving*

*use noodles or rice*

Now, here's the venison version.

## Candlelight Stroganoff (with venison)

1 to 1-1/2 pounds round venison steak, cut into ½-inch strips
2 tablespoons margarine
2 cups onion, sliced and separated (about 3 small onions)
1/2 cup flour
1-1/2 cups beef broth
1/2 cup burgundy cooking wine
3 tablespoons tomato paste
1/2 teaspoon thyme
1/2 teaspoon celery seed
1/4 teaspoon garlic salt
3/4 cup sour cream
hot, cooked and buttered noodles or cooked white rice (just before serving)

In a large, deep skillet, melt margarine and brown meat. Stir in onions, celery seed and garlic salt. Cook for three additional minutes. Remove skillet from heat. Sprinkle flour over meat and stir until well combined. Stir in beef broth, burgundy wine, tomato paste and thyme until blended and smooth. Once mixture is warm, transfer to a crock pot. Cook in crock-pot on High for 2-3 hours until sauce is thickened and begins to boil. Be careful not to scorch. Add more liquid (beef broth) and reduce heat if necessary. Just before serving, stir sour cream into the sauce. Serve over hot buttered noodles or cooked white rice.

Despite it's fancy appearance, this particular recipe didn't really require an extensive amount of reconstructive surgery to make it a beaut with venison. But I think you now have a fairly good idea of just how easy it is to identify a good recipe candidate for venison substitution and modify it accordingly. Now, get out your cookbooks, dust them off, and look for a few potential Bull's Eye Recipes.

## South of the Border Brainstorm

As you venture out and become more brazen in your venison test kitchen, you'll find (as I did) that one creative recipe idea leads to another. While simmering our famous ground venison for *The Best Tacos in Town*, I wondered, "Hmmm, do you suppose I could eke another dish or two out of tonight's leftover taco meat?" By golly, I did! By now, I had not only become accustomed to the aroma of simmering venison, but actually anticipated smelling the celery, garlic, onion and hot sauce as it steeped away in the skillet. When I leaned over to take a big whiff of the Mexican inspired spice combination as it bonded to my ground venison, I took a little trip down memory lane to the first year I lived in my very first apartment. My room-mate happened to be of Brazilian heritage. Since my most "sophisticated" culinary skills at the time resulted in a good pot of macaroni and cheese, we often feasted on South American-inspired dishes that she would whip up in mere minutes. My favorite was a combination of rice, meat (bathed in spices), diced tomatoes and cheese.

For the sake of culinary humanity, Tito, the cat, donated his share of the leftover taco meat for my South American pursuit. I had just enough leftover meat to make a scrumptious lunch for myself the very next day. If the recipe was not a success, Tito would indeed still be heir to the grub. With my sombrero on my head and some Spanish music playing in the background (well, not really…but that would be fun, eh?), I reheated the taco meat in a skillet with some canned diced tomatoes. Some instant rice was boiling away. As soon as both items were done, I put my rice on a plate, layered some sliced American cheese over the rice and topped it off with my new meat mixture. The heat from both the rice and meat mixture melted the cheese perfectly into both. As I sat there and savored my tasty new creation, I thought to myself, "This is way better than any Hamburger Helper mix could ever hope to be, and it took less time!" Tito, the cat, seemed far less im-pressed as he gazed longingly through the window at what was suppose to be his share of the family feast.

## The Venison Dream Team

So, you've successfully prepared some of the recipes I've included to get you started. You've even ventured out and figured out how to identify potential recipes for venison substitution. Congratulations! Now, to get your creative juices really pumped up, imagine yourself perusing cookbooks and recipes just for inspiration. You might create a totally new recipe. I'm not talking about nipping and tucking, but rather major renovations in such a way that the original recipe is but a shadow behind your final result. This creative and imaginative process inspired many, if not most, of my venison appetizer recipes.

Although I had managed to embrace venison in many areas of my cooking, the idea of serving venison appetizers had intimidated me. Oh, I had managed to have some success using ground venison for various cocktail meatballs, but beyond that, I couldn't find anything original or different. Since good venison recipes were scarce (at best), I found appetizer recipes to be virtually non-existent.

So, where did I start? With my imagination. Then I consulted my taste buds who also wisely called upon my memory for a little assistance. With these three trustworthy confidants on my team, I pulled out a few fancy cookbooks, loaded with pictures, and began to make a list of all the things that my imagination, my taste buds and my memory said I would like to have in an appetizer.

One of the first things I stumbled across was Rumaki. Rumaki appetizers consist of chicken liver and water chestnut slices, wrapped up in a piece of bacon, broiled in a teriyaki-type sauce. Perusing the list of ingredients, my taste buds promptly piped up and said, "Chicken livers! Uuuggg! I don't think so!"

But, whoa! My memory charged right in with, "Oh but, don't you recall the time when we ate those deliciously simple morsels of bacon wrapped around a whole water chestnut at the Bible study Christmas party?"

"Oh, right! They too were broiled to a crisp. We do really enjoy the taste and crunch of a whole water chestnut," added my taste buds.

"Uh, huh. I thought so. After all, you wolfed down about 30 of them that night," my memory recalled.

"Oh, Puuleeeasse! I don't think I was that bad," my taste buds tartly replied.

"All right! Time Out!" refereed my imagination. "We've all decided that we know we like bacon wrapped around chestnuts and broiled. Now, can we get down to business and figure out how to tastefully add some venison to the pot?"

My taste buds and my memory put their heads together and finally came up with a suggestion. "We do really like the venison steak marinade. Perhaps we can figure out a way to use the sauce from the marinade to come up with something fun."

"Perhaps," pondered my imagination. "And maybe we can marinate some venison round steak strips. Then, we can wrap the marinated steak strip and the chestnut in bacon and broil it. What do you think gals?"

"Mmmmm, sounds great. Let's go!"

And, that's what we did. I reduced my famous venison steak marinade by half, sliced up a venison round steak into ¼-inch strips and set them to marinate in the refrigerator for about four hours. Of course, that was the easiest part. I still had to assemble and cook them.

The assembly, although messy, went fairly well. I cut a slab of bacon in half. For each appetizer, I laid a piece of steak on the bacon. Then, I placed a whole water chestnut in the center of the steak strip. I rolled it all up and secured it with a round toothpick.

The real tricky part was when I attempted to cook the appetizers. Since I didn't have much experience broiling or cooking with bacon, I consulted the original Rumaki recipe that said to broil the Rumaki 6 inches from the heat, 15 to 20 minutes. So, with that in mind, I put about 12 of my newly created appetizers on a cookie sheet and placed it in my electric oven about 6 inches from the broiler coil. After about 10 minutes, my oven sounded like a firecracker warehouse set ablaze. Dark gray smoke oozed out of the heat exhaust. A new member of my creative dream team, my common sense, told me "Something's not right here!"

I opened the oven door to discover a small light show as my appetizers floated around in hot grease. "Ooops, guess we needed to use a broiler pan," added my common sense. I carefully and quickly pulled out the blazing cookie sheet and transferred my appetizers to a broiler pan…charred toothpicks and all. Another five minutes in the oven and they came out looking beautiful. Too bad the whole house, including my husband's freshly washed and prepared hunting clothes, now smelled like charred bacon. I guess since deer are not normally lured by the smell of bacon, my husband was not very pleased. Nonetheless, I convinced him to take my new creation to work to share with his work buddies. He and the appetizers were a BIG hit! Good thing they didn't notice the charred toothpicks.

Now that my new appetizer was a bona fide success, all I had to do was name it. Huddling with the dream team of my imagination, my taste buds and my memory, we began to brainstorm.

"Why don't we call it Those Bacon and Water Chestnut Thingadoos?" a fine suggestion by my memory.

"Naaahhhh. That's not gonna work," my taste buds hastily replied.

"You didn't say anything about the steak or marinade, which is what makes it so special."

"How about Buck Eyes?" inquired my imagination. "I mean, I know it doesn't say anything about what's in the appetizer…but after all, it is an appetizer so let's give it a fun name."

"Buck Eyes?" Yeah, Buck Eyes. So there you have it. A day in the life of creating a venison appetizer – starring me, my imagination, my taste buds and my memory. And co-starring a bit of common sense.

Another interesting appetizer included in this book, Party Triangles, was inspired only by a picture in a cookbook and a few common ingredients. Practically all of the other ingredients and preparation details were scrapped as I called upon my memory and my taste buds for inspiration. Below is the original recipe and how I completely dissected it and created my own new appetizer.

## Oriental Triangles

1/2 pound lean ground beef *Yuck! use real broth*
1 envelope (1 ounce) beef and mushroom dry soup mix *onion + spice*
1/2 cup sliced water chestnuts, finely chopped *keep*
1 cup canned bean sprouts, drained *scrap*  *add mushrooms – mmm!*
2 tablespoons chopped onion
2 tubes (8 ounces each) refrigerated crescent rolls *make cream cheese filling*
Prepared sweet-and-sour sauce, optional *>make*
Prepared hot mustard sauce, optional *>horseradish instead*

In a skillet, combine first five ingredients. Cook over medium heat, stirring often, until beef is browned and onion is tender. Separate crescent dough into triangles; cut each one in half diagonally. Place one rounded teaspoon of beef mixture in the center of each triangle; fold dough over mixture and pinch corners together to seal edges. Place on an ungreased baking sheet. Bake at 375 degrees for 15 minutes or until golden. Serve with sweet-and-sour sauce and hot mustard sauce if desired.

*These are too small!! use 2 triangles for each appetizer*

# Crescent Party Triangles

4 ounces cream cheese, softened
1/2 egg, beaten (discard other 1/2)
1/4 teaspoon garlic puree
2 tablespoons Parmesan/Romano cheese
1/2 pound ground venison
½ of 5-ounce can of sliced water chestnuts, chopped
½ of 4-ounce can sliced mushrooms, chopped
1/2 teaspoon garlic salt or garlic puree
1/4 teaspoon celery salt
2 teaspoons onion, minced
3 tablespoons beef broth
2 or 3 packages refrigerator crescent rolls

Dipping Sauce:
1/2 cup sour cream
1 teaspoon horseradish sauce

Combine first four ingredients and blend well. Set aside. In a skillet over medium heat, combine venison, chestnuts, mushrooms, garlic salt (or puree), celery salt, onion and broth. Cook until meat is done. Coat a cookie sheet or baking stone with non-stick cooking spray. Place a crescent triangle on the cookie sheet. Spread it with the cream cheese mixture to 1/8-inch of the edge. Spoon about one tablespoon of meat mixture on top of cream cheese spread. Cover with another crescent triangle and seal the edges by crimping with a fork. Repeat until all ingredients have been exhausted. Bake triangles at 375 degrees for 15-18 minutes or until crescent pastry is golden-brown. Combine sour cream and horseradish sauce. Serve with warm triangles. This recipe can be easily doubled for a larger batch.

My husband cautioned me not to use the word "oriental" in my venison recipe titles, claiming that fellow "meat and potatoes" types might snarl at such a title. Like most "meat and potatoes" men I've met, he just does not appreciate chow-meiney, bean-sprouty, pea-poddin types of ingredients added to his food. Using the word 'oriental' might imply there will be lots of these unwelcome and unknown ingredients hidden inside the triangle pocket. In all the years I've attempted to force feed my husband new and different recipes of international flavor, about the only "oriental" ingredient he's managed to fully appreciate is the water chestnut (which, coincidentally is included in this recipe). I, on the other hand, adore Asian cuisine. So I couldn't resist including a few recipes. I hope you enjoy them.

Well, it came down to an arm wrestling match to see who would name the recipe. My husband on one side with the sensible name of *Crescent Party Triangles*. I on the other with the more culturally flavored *Oriental Pockets*. You guessed it. He won and Party Triangles it is. Guess I should spend more time in the gym, eh? Nahhh! Next time I'll just dab a little oleo on the table under his elbow.

After a few years of cooking and experimenting in the kitchen with venison, I found myself becoming, much to the delight of my family, more creative, bold and brazen in other areas of my cooking. I trust by now you have concluded that the options you have with venison are endless! No longer brainwashed by the myth that you have to "mask" the auspicious wild flavor of venison, you can now embrace it and use it to prepare feast after delicious feast for your friends and family. After investing the time and energy it took to read this entire chapter you may find yourself challenged, inspired and full of anticipation for what new recipe you'll whip up next. If so, I encourage you to share your blessing with others in your community. Call your local community college (or community center) and offer to teach a class on venison cooking. You'll be amazed how many folks turn out to hear what you have to say and taste what you have prepared!

# LETS GET TO WORK!

# Tips, Tricks And Tools of The Trade

So you've mustered up enough courage to open the little white package, marked "WILD GAME - NOT FOR SALE!!" and you survived. Good! I knew you would. Before you toss your venison in the skillet, let me share a few tips, tricks and tools of the trade that will make your kitchen encounters with venison even more enjoyable.

## What's So Special About Celery, Onion And Garlic?

    As I mentioned in Chapter 1, celery, onion and garlic are three dependable divas that almost always play some sort of supporting role in my venison dishes. Occasionally, I'll cast in a few green peppers, but celery, onion and garlic remain the big three. If we take a closer look at each vegetable, you'll understand why they play such a vital role in many of my recipes.

**Celery:** For much of the same reason celery ends up on most dieters' plates, it ends up in my recipes. Celery is composed of 95 percent water! In addition to it's powerful flavor, freshly minced or chopped celery often adds much-needed moisture, in lieu of heavy oils or other fat substitutions, to properly simmer the low-fat venison. Minced celery, when simmered with ground venison, blends well with the meat to create a finely textured meat mixture. When fresh celery is not readily handy, celery salt and celery seed are also honorable venison flavor-enhancers, although they don't provide the moisture. In all forms, celery plays an important aromatic role in the cooking pot.

Celery Math:
>     1 teaspoon celery salt = 1 ½ to 2 stalks of celery (and you can
>         probably reduce or omit any additional salt in recipe)
>     1/2 teaspoon celery seed = 1 ½ to 2 stalks of celery
>     2 stalks celery = approximately 1/2 cup minced
>     2 stalks celery = approximately 1 cup chopped

**Onion:** When it comes to onion, what is irritating to the eyes is succulent for the venison, especially the steak cuts. Why? Because when you slice an onion, you've got a little chemistry experiment going on right there in your kitchen. The onion releases a few enzymes that attack these poor pathetic and passive sulfur compounds. This act of warfare creates volatile acids and ammonia which causes our eyes to uncontrollably and forcibly spit tears. This also happens to produce the onion's wonderfully strong flavor and natural tenderizing properties.

Since onions are used in the cooking of practically every country in the world, it's no wonder I've included them as one of the top three indispensable vegetable flavorings for venison. Without onions, many dishes would be flavorless. Though there are various forms of onion flavoring such as onion flakes, onion salt and onion powder, I often prefer to use freshly chopped or minced (or frozen varieties). Much like celery, onions also add essential moisture to your venison recipe. Later in this chapter I'll offer some quick little preparation tips that will help keep you well-stocked in freshly chopped and/or minced celery and onion.

Onion Math:

 1 small = 1/3 cup chopped
 1 medium = 1/2 cup chopped
 1 large = 1 cup chopped

**Garlic:** The most pungent of the three spice divas, garlic often plays a small yet powerfully aromatic role in venison cookery. Garlic, a close relative of the onion, also releases volatile compounds (of the oily sort) when chopped, or more profoundly, when crushed or smashed. Since I've already stressed the virtues of using fresh celery and fresh onion, you might very well assume that I use nothing but freshly chopped or minced garlic, eh? On the contrary. I'm almost ashamed to admit that I've only held a genuine garlic clove maybe once or twice in my life and I don't own a garlic press. Why? Because standing over the stove, frantically trying to peel a tiny garlic glove with my klutzy fingers while my toddler tugs away at my leg for her fifth glass of juice in the past 20 minutes is just not my idea of fun. As often as I use garlic in my kitchen, repeating this scenario would definitely result in one mean mamma in search of her sanity. Instead, I opt for my faithful jar of garlic puree or bottled minced garlic and a trusty teaspoon. The baby gets her juice, I keep my sanity and the garlic lands in the skillet with the simmering venison.

For those of you who are accustomed to using fresh garlic, by all means continue doing so. I applaud your God-given talent, skill and patience in the kitchen. For the rest of you (me included), look for bottled garlic puree or bottled minced garlic in your produce section. It should be displayed in or around the onions, garlic and ginger. Unless otherwise specified in the recipe, opt for the bottled minced or pureed garlic over other forms of garlic such as dried minced garlic, garlic salt or garlic powder. But any of these three will do in a pinch.

Garlic Math:

> 1 fresh clove = 1/2 teaspoon bottled minced or pureed garlic
> 1 fresh clove = 1/8 teaspoon dried minced garlic or garlic powder
> 1 fresh clove = 1 teaspoon garlic salt (you can probably reduce or omit any additional salt in recipe)
> 1 teaspoon garlic salt = 1/8 teaspoon garlic powder plus 7/8 teaspoon salt

## Stress-Saving Tips For The Venison Cook

Ever found yourself in a pinch with little or no time to chop an onion, a green pepper or a few celery stalks? Do you rummage through your refrigerator looking for celery only to find that it has turned into a rubber plant? Or, do you find yourself not bothering to buy fresh onion, celery or green pepper because you never seem to completely use them before they become unrecognizable fuzzy objects? Give yourself a break and use some of these time-saving and stress-saving tips.

- •After you use a portion of an onion for your current recipe, seal the rest of the onion in an airtight container and store it in your refrigerator. If you haven't used the rest of it in 2 to 3 days, chop it up and store it in a freezer bag in the freezer. Frozen onions will keep their freshness for about 10 to 12 months at 0 degrees F. If you don't trust yourself and think you might forget about the onion in the refrigerator, immediately chop and store the remaining onion in the freezer.

- •Before your celery stalks turn into rubbery pogo sticks, chop them and store in a freezer bag in the freezer. If you find it hard to keep track of the status of your celery, simply chop half of the celery bunch for freezer storage right after you get it home from the grocery store. Celery will keep its freshness in the freezer for about three months.

•It is less often that I use green pepper in my venison cooking, but, when I need it, I *really* need it. That's usually about two days after I just threw away a barely recognizable green pepper that previously lived somewhere in the back of my vegetable crisper. Since most of my recipes call for chopped green pepper, I generally seed and chop the green goblets as soon as I get them home from the grocery or as soon as I harvest them from my garden. I don't even kid myself anymore because I know I'm not organized enough to use my green peppers before they expire. Frozen green pepper will keep its freshness for about six months.

•If a recipe calls for minced onion or minced celery and all you have is your frozen chopped variety, use the chopped. It's a recipe, not a regulation. If you still insist on mincing your celery and onion, run a little warm water over the frozen pieces until defrosted enough to run through your mini-chopper.

•If you want to be really prepared, go one step further and freeze some minced or finely chopped onion and celery. My mother-in-law taught me this simple tip. She places about two tablespoons of minced or finely chopped onion or celery in a little folded packet of tin foil. Then, when she needs some, but doesn't have fresh, she grabs as many foil packets as she needs and runs them under hot water to defrost the frozen mini-block of spice.

The next time you need chopped or minced onion or celery or chopped green pepper in a jiffy, grab a handful or two from your frozen stash. If your frozen, chopped vegetables stick together a bit, just give the bag a whack on the counter to break them up. Depending on your situation, I'm sure you'll find one or more of these time-saving tips useful in your venison cooking. I found that I couldn't survive without them.

## Simple Simmering And Browning Techniques

Simmering and browning venison sounds like an easy enough thing to do, right? Well, maybe, but not if you apply the same principles as you would when you simmer and brown beef. Silly as it sounds, some of the things we would ordinarily and naturally do when simmering beef, can, when applied to venison, adversely affect the outcome of your venison meal.

For example, never fry ground venison over high heat so as to quickly brown the meat. Instead, *simmer* it slowly over medium heat so that it has time to bond with all the wonderful spices and flavors included in the skillet. As you simmer the ground venison, continually stir and work the meat using your spatula until it becomes a very fine, crumbled texture ripe and ready to be added to your recipe. Compare this to fried beef which generally ends up as lumpy, generously sized, gristly chunks of meat.

In our enlightened health conscious society, we are always told to drain any and all fat (lest it end up on our hips or stuffed in our arteries) after we brown our beef. Not so with venison. To do so would be a tragic mistake. The liquid (not to be confused with fat) that results from simmering ground venison has been provided compliments of your fresh onion, celery or other fresh ingredients added to the skillet. Some of this liquid is the natural moisture found in the venison. If you have added ground pork to your ground venison during processing, a very small percentage of this liquid may include fat from pork.

The venison, along with the celery, onion, garlic and other spices, simmer together to create a strong, robust broth that becomes a very essential element to the overall flavor of your venison entree. If you taste a spoonful of this tasty broth, you'll see what I mean and why it would be such a tragedy to exclude it from the rest of the cooking process.

An interesting little bit of trivia about ground venison, especially if you are going to try using it in a recipe that normally calls for ground beef: one pound of venison is one pound of simmered and fully cooked venison. One pound of beef is roughly 3/4 pound or less of simmered and fully cooked ground beef, depending on the quality and fat content of the beef you normally use. If your recipe calls for one pound of ground beef, unless you enjoy an abundance of meat in your recipe, use a little less venison than the beef recipe calls for. One pound of venison is suitable for any recipe that calls for 1-1/2 pounds of beef.

When a recipe calls for you to simmer and brown venison steaks, again, you will do so slowly over medium heat thus allowing the steaks to absorb the flavor of the onion, celery, garlic or other spices. As you simmer the steaks, cover the skillet with a lid, turning the steaks as needed to get the job done. It may be necessary to turn down the heat just a little bit. The additional heat and steam, along with the added moisture from the vegetables, penetrates the meat and breaks down the tougher tissues of the venison steak so it will better absorb the flavors. It really doesn't take any longer to brown and simmer venison steaks than it does to simmer ground venison, because the additional heat and steam aid in hastening the browning process.

If a recipe calls for you to brown and simmer ground venison patties, grab your skillet lid and use the same principle as you would with venison steaks.

## Quick Defrosting For The Venison Cook

If you are anything at all like me, you often find yourself deciding what to fix for dinner one hour (or less) before dinner is suppose to be on the table. So, what do you do when all your venison is a solid block of ice and the time is ticking away?

You just walked in the door, the kids are screaming for *The Best Tacos in Town* and you forgot to pull out the ground venison from the freezer last night. Before you do anything else, fill up a bowl (preferably a stainless steel bowl) with the hottest tap water you can get out of the faucet. Submerge your package of ground venison and let it soak while you change clothes or hear your child's play-by-play of the day's activities. After about five minutes, dump the old water and run some more hot tap water. Soak for another five minutes. By now, a good portion of the ground venison should be defrosted. Remove the plastic packaging and scrape the softened meat away from the remaining frozen meat, and throw it in the skillet. Depending on how large the frozen section is, either throw it in the skillet and let it thaw as it cooks, or zap it in the microwave on high for about one minute or until it has softened up enough to break it up into smaller pieces.

I generally prefer the quick-soaking last-minute defrost method over depending wholly on the microwave's defrosting capabilities. Though I must admit, they have vastly improved the technology. I brought home my first microwave only to watch my roommate explode a Pop Tart in it. On the few occasions I attempt to take full advantage of the slick defrosting capabilities of my new model, I must watch it like a hawk or I'll find a shriveled lump of meat that looks and smells like an old shoe!

When using the convenience of a microwave to defrost my ground venison, I employ a few little tricks that help maintain the meat's original composition. You may want to refer to the instruction manual for your specific model before you attempt to imitate my microwave defrosting technique.

Despite its awesome appearance, I still haven't figured out how to completely control my technologically advanced microwave. So I just use the nine or ten pre-programmed buttons that are provided for those of us who do not wish to enroll in a class for the Microwave-challenged. After placing my packaged ground venison on a microwave-safe plate inside the microwave, I locate the preset button labeled GROUND MEAT DEFROST 1/2 LB. Hey! Can't go wrong there, eh? Well, that's what I thought. I press this button for however many 1/2 pounds there are in my package. For a one-pound package, I press it twice. Then, my mighty microwave sprints into action, lights up, spins the turntable and begins to alternately high-zap and low-zap my ground venison. After doing this for about a minute and a half, it beckons my attention with a few annoying, repetitive beeps. The display tells me I need to "PULL APART, REMOVE". At this point, I remove the plastic covering and check to see if any of the ground venison has softened. If so, I scrape off the softened portion, set it aside, and turn the meat over. Returning the remaining frozen ground venison to the micro-wave, I press the start button so that it can continue defrosting. In another couple of minutes, it beeps again and I scrape off more soft meat. At this point, when you place the remaining frozen portion in the microwave (turned over again), keep an eye on the progress, it may not take as long as the microwave has assumed it would to finish the job. If you are not careful, you may still end up with a shriveled up, stinky piece of meat (albeit smaller) that looks like an old shoe.

You can also use either quick-defrosting method for venison steaks. When using the quick-soak method, first remove the outer paper packaging from the steaks. Sometimes there will also be a thin, plastic sheet between each steak. Leave it for now.

After the first five minutes of soaking, drain the cold water and try to separate the steaks and remove the thin plastic sheet, if possible. Soak in another bowl of hot water for another five minutes. If necessary, repeat one more time, but be careful that the water is not hot enough to actually "brown" the meat at this point.

If you choose to use the microwave, use the same cautions I mentioned for defrosting ground venison, lest you end up with an old, stinky piece of leather. When the microwave beckons your attention, check to see if you can pry the meat apart and remove the thin plastic liners. Turn over the meat and return to the microwave for another blast. Repeat until steaks are nearly (nearly is good enough) defrosted, turning them over each time. Be sure to keep any eye on those last few minutes.

If your microwave does not have any type of "automatic" defrost feature, try zapping the meat at half-power for about 1 1/2 to 2 minutes at a time, scraping and/or turning as you go, until the meat is ready to cook.

If, in the process of thawing or defrosting your venison, blood seeps out of the meat, discard the blood. Including it in your skillet does not enhance the overall flavor of your recipe. It may reduce the moisture somewhat, but you can add that back in with a tablespoon or two of hot water.

## Moonlight Marinating Tips

I am always astounded when I run across any type of recipe, though they are more frequently found in wild game recipes, that call for marathon marinating times of more than 24 hours. Some even suggest soaking the meat for 2 to 3 days! I don't know about you, but any kind of unpreserved meat that happens to be in my refrigerator a breath longer than 2 days is immediately discharged. No questions asked!

Depending on the cut of meat you are marinating, anywhere from 6 to 8 hours is sufficient marinating time to both tenderize and flavor the meat. If it is a tougher cut, prepare the marinade the evening before your meal and allow the meat to marinate overnight and until you begin to prepare dinner. Sauerbraten is about the only exception. Minimum marinating time for ground meat and steak strips is two hours.

## Substituting Ground Venison For Steak, And Steak For Ground Venison

So, what do you do if you really, really want to fix a recipe that calls for cube steaks or tenderloins or some other venison steak cut and the only thing left in the deep freeze is ground venison? Don't sweat it. Be flexible and reorient your thinking. When contemplating the bold (yet brave) idea of substituting one cut of meat for another, use the following checklist to determine the feasibility and game plan.

_____ Instead of using steaks, can I use ground venison patties and still achieve a similar meal using the same or similar cooking methods as described in the recipe?

_____ If the recipe calls for cooking steaks in a crock pot, if I use ground venison, can I reduce my crock pot cooking time or simply cook it in a skillet or in the oven?

_____ Instead of steak, can I use ground venison in this recipe to create a sandwich or skillet meal (i.e., Sloppy Joes, BBQ, Italian Sandwiches, Fajitas, stir fry, etc.)

_____ Does it appear that I can use ground venison in soup instead of diced steak?

_____ Or, instead of ground venison, can I use cubed steaks and cook them just a little longer to allow the steak to tenderize and absorb the flavors?

_____ Or, instead of ground venison, can I use an arm steak or round steak with this gravy or in this soup?

If you answered YES to one or more of these questions, you can probably do it! Keep in mind, however, that not all recipes can easily interchange ground venison and venison steaks. But, many will.

For example, Fajitas seem more authentic using steak strips, but you will still enjoy the same flavor using ground venison. Don't have a desire to put diced bits of venison steak in your vegetable soup? Use ground venison. It works just as well or better. In my experience I've also found that ground venison patties marinade quite well. If the marinade does not completely cover the patties, simply turn the patties over half way through the marinating time. I encourage you not to overlook the various wonderful marinade recipes in the market simply because you have run out of venison steaks or because you don't have the specific cut called for in the recipe. Put your imagination and ingenuity to work and defrost your ground venison. You'll be glad you did.

## Essential Venison Kitchen Tools

Quite possibly revered even more highly than the mighty microwave, my faithful crock pots (I own three) have dutifully cooked countless tasty, tender meat entrees, many of them containing venison, while I was working outside the home managing a marketing department for a multi-million dollar computer distributor. Now that I am at home, managing a multi-faceted household (though, less financially impressive), I still manage to keep these workhorse crock pots very busy.

By utilizing a "low-watt blanket of heat" and a glass lid to hold in moisture, crock pots have revolutionized the way we cook tougher cuts of roasts and steaks (including venison) and are great for cooking a hearty, healthy pot of soup or stew. It has been my personal experience that with a little preparation and planning, venison responds gracefully to the "fill and forget" method of crock pot cooking. It's like having the convenience of marinating and long roasting all in one little steamy, stoneware package. Although crock pots are not based on rocket science technology, you do need to spend some time becoming familiar with their cooking nuances. I have three different crock pots. One is a 3-1/2- quart model another that holds a mighty 5 quarts, and a small 1-quart (one temperature) model. The two larger models both have two temperatures settings: LOW and HIGH. Much like my children, these pots behave in very different ways. One tends to cook a little hotter (and thus, quicker) on HIGH than it's compadre crock. My 1-quart model only has one temperature setting (LOW), but due to its small size, it cooks as fast as the larger models on HIGH. If you have little or no experience working with a crock pot, here are a few tips that should help warm you up to the crock pot way of life:[1]

Most crock pots are equipped with two temperature settings - LOW and HIGH. Low is for slow "all-day" cooking. One hour on High equals about 2 to 2-1/2 hours on Low.

Almost all crock pot cooking requires liquid (there are very few exceptions), but when adapting a recipe to the crock pot, you may need less liquid than a recipe normally calls for. The slow-cooking method retains more juices in meats and vegetables than in conventional cooking. Also, liquids tend not to "boil away" as in conventional cooking. You'll often have more liquid at the end of cooking instead of less.

## Crock Pot Math

| If Recipe Says: | Cook on Low | or | Cook on High |
|---|---|---|---|
| 15 to 30 minutes | 4 to 6 hours | | 1 ½ to 2 hours |
| 35 to 45 minutes | 6 to 10 hours | | 3 to 4 hours |
| 50 minutes to 3 hours | 8 to 18 hours | | 4 to 6 hours |

The chart above offers some helpful guidelines, but it still does not replace personal experience with your crock pot. If, after slow-cooking your meal all day long on LOW, you come home to discover that it is still not quite done, simply turn it up to HIGH to finish cooking during the next hour or so while you change clothes, set the table and catch up on family communication.

Another equally indispensable tool in my venison kitchen is an electric mini-chopper, an inexpensive yet modern appliance. I personally use a Black and Decker Handy Chopper my mother-in-law gave me for Christmas several years ago. However, I understand there are loads of brand names and chopper models to choose from ranging in costs anywhere from $20 on up. If you don't already own one of these efficient, time-saving kitchen tools, do yourself a favor and run down to your local discount superstore and buy one! You'll be glad you did.

So, what's so special about this modern day chopper, you might ask? Well, I have to confess that even though many of my recipes call for diced or chopped ingredients, such as onion and celery, if I am short on time, patience, creativity or sanity that day (which is quite often, I'm sorry to say), I pull out the handy chopper. I stuff as many cut up chunks of onion and celery (why do it in two steps if I don't have to?) into the chopper, press the red button, and let her rip! The result isn't a bunch of perfectly cut squares of vegetables, but it is chopped and it works, really well, really fast! Get the picture? I use our chopper so much it has earned itself preferred seating right on top of my microwave, dutifully waiting to serve.

## Last But Not Least, Be Flexible!

Do you find yourself needlessly waiting to cook venison, making excuses because you don't have an ingredient listed in the recipe? Please keep in mind this is Venison Cooking 101, not culinary parochial school. Sister Gourmet is not going to come along and whack your knuckles for breaking the rules. As the author of this book and these recipes, I grant you full permission to break any rules you want so you can have a satisfying meal in a reasonable amount of time. Now, bear in mind that chili won't taste very much like chili without chili powder. Otherwise, feel free to nip and tuck and substitute away.

[1] Adapted from the Rival® Crock Pot Stoneware Slow Cooker Instruction Manual. CROCK-POT is a registered trademark of The Rival Company.

"FAMILY, MEET MR. DEER."

# Introducing Venison To Your Family

Suppose you've never once cooked a meal with venison for your family and you are ready to do so now. What do you fix? What's the best way to impress them with your newfound venison culinary skills?

Do yourself a favor. Don't announce to the clan that you've finally figured out how to cook venison and your going to start with some fancy, shmancy recipe they've never heard of. Such an announcement may only serve to inspire mutiny within the household which could end with the troops commandeering the family vehicle for a trip to the nearest fast food joint.

The easiest way to introduce venison to your family without abusing their limited willingness to try something new, is to fix them something they already like. For example, if they enjoy chili, fix chili with venison. If they enjoy meatloaf, fix a venison meatloaf. If, after you serve the meal, they inquire about any subtle differences they may notice, simply announce that you found a new chili (or meatloaf) recipe and you would love to hear how they like it.

Just because you are now cooking with venison, doesn't mean your family has to know all the details about what's in a recipe. Think about it for a minute. How often do you give our family a play-by-play rundown of all the ingredients in any recipe you cook, much less a new one? Please don't misunderstand what I am suggesting. If asked point blank if there is venison in the meal, don't lie. Not only is lying a terrible character flaw, but it may actually make matters worse.

After your family has responded positively to your new recipe for chili or meatloaf (or whatever), now is the time to let them in on your secret. If they had a pleasant experience, they'll walk away from the table remembering these three things:

1. I liked the meal.

2. It had venison in it.

3. I think I like venison.

If, however, nobody seemed to like your new recipe and most of it went untouched, don't automatically assume it was because of the venison. It may have been because the flavors are just not their cup of tea. Simply thank your family for being patient in trying your new recipe. Let them know you'll try to find a better recipe next time. Now is definitely not the time to tell them there was venison in the pot. Otherwise, they'll walk away from the table remembering *these* three things:

1. That was a terrible meal!

2. It had venison in it.

3. I definitely don't like venison!

## Kids And Venison

I am often asked "How do you get your kids to eat venison?" To which I reply, "Well, how do you get your kids to eat beef?" As they tilt their head in puzzlement, I continue "You cook it in spaghetti, or tacos, on pizza, in between a hamburger bun or purchase it in a bag labeled 'Kid's Meal' and serve it up on the table, right?" As they nod their head in agreement, I continue.

"And, when you do this, you don't make a point to announce that it's beef on the table for dinner do you? If you feel compelled to announce the dinner menu, you simply tell them they are eating spaghetti (or whatever you're fixing that night) for dinner tonight, right?"

I guess I'm always a bit surprised by these questions, because our children have always eaten venison. Our eldest probably started eating it at about age 3 and our youngest started eating it as soon as she was able to eat solid foods. Lots of neighborhood kids and classmates have eaten venison at our house without any complaints. They gobble it right up without ever knowing they were eating venison. We just never made a big deal about it.

But, suppose venison has not been a staple of your family diet and your children are much older, much wiser, and are a bit squeamish at the thought of eating deer meat, or worse, Bambi!! What do you do?

If you have already tried all my suggestions thus far for introducing venison to your family and you still have a staunch protester in the family, read on for some helpful negotiating tips.

Although our 7-year-old has no qualms about eating venison, that doesn't mean she has no heart for the welfare of animals. In fact, we often drive through a nearby state park on our way to town to enjoy the breathtaking beauty of several herds of deer browsing in the forest. She loves watching the deer. She delights in their grace, form and beauty even though she knows these same animals eventually end up on her plate in the form of spaghetti and taco meat.

Given the opportunity to frequently observe deer and their behaviors, she also understands how well God equipped the deer with excellent survival skills such as a strong sense of smell, superior hearing, speed and agility. She does not see the deer as a frail, helpless victim, but rather as a challenging opponent for her father's sport of hunting. We've taught her not to confuse her love, appreciation and respect for nature and animals with worship for nature and animals.

With all of this in mind, I do realize the impact that one simple, yet touching, animated Walt Disney film had on an entire generation, and its children. According to some sources I've read, the year prior to the release of *Bambi*, the deer hunting industry in the United States was a $9.5 million business. In 1942, Walt Disney released *Bambi*. The following season, deer hunters spent only $4.1 million on tags, permits and hunting trips.[1]

So, how do you undo this brainwashing of your impressionable child? Paint an emotional word picture that will help them understand how impractical their theory and reasoning for not eating venison actually is. That's right, use the same theory that put them in this place to begin with. That should help to set them back on the right course. It might also help to remind them that *Bambi* is only a cartoon. It is not real life. That's not how animals in the forest really act.

The next time your children crave their favorite dish or fast food meal that happens to include beef (or another type of commercial meat), try this approach. I'll use tacos and beef as an example.

"Hey Mom! I'm dying to have tacos tonight? Can we go to town and get some?" suggests your 12-year-old, highly metabolic, carbohydrate-consuming, protein-starved child.

"Gosh, hon…I don't know. You see, I stopped by this farm the other day and watched a few cattle graze in the fields. One of them walked over and, well, we sort of hit it off. Then, along came her calf and oh, I just fell in love with him! After having this emotional encounter with these two cows, I don't think I could ever eat beef again. I mean, after all, I could very well be eating that poor calf's mother!!"

Now, keep in mind that this type of reverse psychology is best if used on children who have already reached adolescence. They have to be old enough to understand the irony laced with a touch of sarcasm. If you try this on kids who are much younger than this, you might wind up with a tearful child who won't eat any meat. Then again, a much younger child is more likely to eat whatever you serve on her plate without giving you the venison inquisition.

Unfortunately, I don't have all the answers for converting kids to venison. But, hopefully I've given you a few pointers that will help you redirect their fears and ignorance (as in lack of knowledge, not stupidity) regarding venison. However, if you happen to come up with another creative or more effective method, do let me know and I'll pass it along.

[1] *Hunting Licenses and Federal Deer Stamp Sales as Reported by the Information Bureau of the Department of Interior July 15, 1941 through 1942* (Washington, D.C.: U.S. Fish and Wildlife Bureau, Federal Aid Office, 1942).

# Processing Venison For Your Taste Buds

In this chapter, I am going to talk about how to process venison for your taste buds. For many years, I had taken for granted the pleasant palatability of our venison. That is, until we tried someone else's venison. Some close relatives of ours graciously offered us some of their surplus venison that had been personally butchered by the hunter. Not thinking twice about it, I naively accepted their offering and assumed "Venison is venison, right?"

Wrong! Though it's not totally clear to me just exactly what went wrong, somewhere between the time this deer was killed, field dressed, aged, butchered and stored, something happened. One thing was very clear, this particular harvest was not suitable to represent venison at my dining room table.

After experiencing a few (just a few) traumatic taste bud experiences with venison of unknown origin, I've come to the conclusion that much of my success in cooking and enjoying our venison is due, in large part, to the professional services of our meat processor. It has been my experience that for those who claim to not like the wild taste of venison have never tried venison that was properly handled, aged and processed. When these steps are done correctly, regardless of whether they were done professionally by a meat processor or independently by the hunter, venison will taste good.

Since I directly attribute the high quality of taste in our venison to our meat processor, Hartrich Meats, I decided to visit the shop in Ste. Marie, Illinois to find out as much as I could about processing venison and share it with you.

Nestled in a tiny village of roughly 300 people, Hartrich Meats has been in business serving Jasper County, Illinois and the surrounding areas since 1953 processing beef, pork and venison. After touring the impressive facility, it is easy to understand why folks drive from distant lands to seek out their services. Rumor has it the folks at Hartrich Meats know their stuff and they do it quite well.

My tour guide, Mark Hartrich, began by escorting me to the area where they receive all deer that are to be processed. Upon arrival, the deer is skinned, washed out twice and singed of any and all remaining hair. Each deer is tagged for owner identification and retains its tag throughout the processing. This ensures the hunter will receive the venison he brought in. From that point the carcass goes to a cooler that holds only venison and is maintained or aged at a controlled temperature and humidity until ready to be processed. As a state-licensed and inspected meat processing facility, Hartrich Meats is required to adhere to strict guidelines for storing and processing wild game separate from the inspected meats, such as beef and pork. Within four to seven days, the venison is custom processed (cut into steaks, tenderized, ground into burger, cooked into sausage) per the hunter's specifications. All the meat is wrapped, marked accordingly and stored in the freezer until the customer comes to pick it up.

Mark also pointed out the very high-tech, state-of-the art smoke house that is used to cook and smoke the venison sausage. A microprocessor (a big word for a tiny computer), automatically injects the liquid smoke and adjusts the temperature and humidity of the smoke house based on the internal temperature and humidity levels of the meat until it delivers a juicy, tasty, fully cooked sausage product. Wow! I was impressed.

Throughout our tour, Mark enthusiastically shared a few observations and helpful suggestions for any hunter who is interested in processing venison for their taste buds.

## Taste Bud Tips For The Hunter

- Place your shot in the lung/heart area of a healthy, unstressed deer, so you don't puncture the intestinal tract with the bullet or arrow. When field dressing your deer, take precautions not to puncture the urethra or the intestinal tract with your knife.

- Immediately remove your deer from the woods to a clean environment where it can be field dressed and thoroughly washed with fresh, clean water. Dirt, debris, dried blood and hair all contribute to any trace of wild or foul taste and unsanitary meat.

- Since proper aging of meat only works when both the temperature (below 40° F) and the humidity are controlled, get your carcass (preferably unskinned) to the meat processor as soon as possible.

- Most meat processors can only safely and properly process a certain number of deer per day or week. To ensure a "spot" for your deer, get it there as quickly as you can, especially during those busy, yet short, gun seasons. Although venison processing is a nice little bumper crop of profits in addition to their day-to-day business, state-licensed processors usually wind up working well into the wee hours of the night in order to adhere to strict guidelines and deliver you a quality product. Most self-respecting meat processors won't compromise their license or their reputation to take in an extra $60 or $80, especially if they are paying 1/2 of that in overtime to deliver the meat. Keep this in mind.

- Young bucks (not more than 2 to 3 years old) and does make the best-tasting venison. Older, rutty bucks are better off processed into various types of sausage, such as cooked salami, cooked hot sticks (much like a Slim Jim salami stick), Polish sausage, Italian sausage, bratwurst and bologna.

- Have as much fat trimmed off the meat as possible.

- Have the processor tenderize or *cube* (processed through the tenderizer twice, once each direction) tougher steak cuts, such as those from the back legs or round steaks.

- Have the processor add 20 percent pork (80 percent lean) to your ground venison. In all the years Mark has been processing venison, he has found this to be the most favorable blend. I love my ground venison. So I would have to agree!

- Use your venison within one year of processing. Storing venison in the freezer much longer than one year will begin to decrease the overall taste quality.

## The Perks Of Professional Processing

Taste buds aside, there are a few other reasons why I so highly recommend investing a small amount of money to have your venison commercially processed. For starters, as the cook of this family, I can be certain I won't have any unidentifiable frozen slabs or chunks of meat wasting space in my freezer. The last thing I want is to defrost a chunk of meat only to discover that I don't have a clue as to what cut I have or how to go about cooking it.

A friend of mine who lives down the road told me about her husband who was quite frustrated one day after defrosting a package of meat he thought was venison liver. His family sent it home with him after a recent visit. Anticipating a savory, simmering skillet of venison liver and onions, he was quite disappointed to discover some sort of venison roast (not clearly identifiable) in the wrapper. Somebody else, who will be expecting the roast, must have received the liver.

When you have your venison commercially processed, it is professionally butchered and wrapped in portions according to the specifications you have instructed. What you receive are several little white packages of venison that are clearly marked

Lastly, one of the grandest of all perks is the variety of cuts and processing that are available from a professional meat processor. The cuts and options we benefit the most from include:

- Ground venison burger – Many of my recipes call for ground venison. I find ground venison to be the most versatile and most palatable of all the venison cuts. Although you could produce a similar product with a hand-cranked meat grinder and several hours of your day, you'll likely wind up with a bit of tendonitis after squeezing out a mere 5 or 10 pounds. If you plan to mix in some pork, you may find that the two meats don't bond well. The mixer used by meat processors extracts the proteins in both meats which helps them bond together and with any additional seasonings.

•Tenderized and cubed steaks – A good portion of my recipes call for cubed venison steaks. These steaks, usually from the back leg of the deer, have been run through the tenderizer teeth (that's what they look like) twice, once in each direction. All the repressed anger in the world coupled with a mallet could not tenderize a cut of steak as well as this modern technology. I find these steaks beautifully absorb any kind of marinade, sauce or gravy they are cooked in, thus enhancing the flavor. They also don't need to be cooked an inordinately long time to be tasty.

•Special cuts you request (roasts, round steaks, tenderloins, stew meat) – We enjoy using the arm roasts for Italian sandwiches or big pots of BBQ. Though we cook with them less frequently, the round steaks work wonderfully with any marinade recipe. The tenderloin is the most tender cut – we marinate them for flavor more than for the sake of tenderizing them.

Other processing cuts and options include: Processing with or without the bone – I am told, that many processors prefer to processes bone-out because deer bones are hard and literally eat saw blades. Though they are hard, once cooked, they are also brittle and splinter easily. A strong word of caution not to give deer bones to your pets.

Most processors trim all the excess fat, but be sure to check and request this when you discuss your processing options with your processor. Fat contributes to a gamy taste and shortens the freezer life of your venison.

Last but not least, there are plenty of sausage options. Although there are as many as 60 different sausage seasoning options to pick from, the most commonly requested sausages are cooked salami and salami sticks, cooked Polish sausage, fresh Italian sausage, fresh bratwurst and bologna.

## Checklist For Choosing A Processor

Although you should be able to assume a certain level of quality with a state-licensed meat processor, there are also many highly regarded wild game only processors, which in some states are not required to be licensed. Since reputation rules supreme in assuring you'll be pleased with your final product, check with friends, relatives or area residents who have used their local meat processor to find out if they have been pleased with the meat they have received.

- •Does the meat processor have the necessary facilities to control temperature and humidity to properly age your meat?

- •Does the processor offer a variety of processing options, such as ground venison burger (with or without added pork), tenderizing, cubing and sausage?

- •Is the processor willing to cut and wrap your meat according to the portions you want in each package?

- •Does the processor have a secure tag or tracking system in place to ensure you receive venison from your deer and not someone else's?

- •Can the processor cape the head (if desired) properly for the taxidermist? Will the tag or tracking system ensure that you receive your deer head?

I do realize that for various reasons, not everyone has the option of having their venison commercially processed. And, some folks would just prefer to process their own. Since we have always had our venison commercially processed, I don't have any personal experiences or advice to share with you on the art of butchering and processing your own venison. Thankfully, there are several resources available for those of you who wish to pursue processing your own venison or who would like to improve upon your own technique. I've listed a few in the appendix. Regardless of what route you choose, I hope you wind up with venison worthy and suitable of you and your family's taste buds.

# Hunters For The Hungry

*Blessed are those who are generous, because they feed the poor.*
*(Proverbs 22:9 NLT)*

Before we venture into the kitchen, tie on our aprons and roll up our sleeves, I would like to share some information with you about a nationwide program that helps to feed those who are hungry, underfed or otherwise might not be able to adequately feed their families

Although my initial motivation for writing this book was to share how I am able to use venison, as I prepared to write the first few lines I paused to pray for a bit of guidance and inspiration.

In the week that followed, I learned of a program here in Illinois called *Illinois Sportsmen Against Hunger*. When I called the Illinois Department of Natural Resources (the department that regulates the program), I also discovered that almost every state in America had a similar program under such names as *Sportsmen Against Hunger, Hunters for the Hungry,*

*Buckmasters Project Venison, Whitetails Unlimited* or some variation thereof. For the sake of simplicity, throughout this section, I'll generally refer to these programs as *Hunters for the Hungry*.

I'm not aware of your individual situation, but I can assume that you have been or will be eating venison and you likely have a hunter in the household or in the immediate family. With this in mind, I would like to present the following information about the *Hunters for the Hungry* program. It is my hope that after reading this material you will "...Give whatever you can according to what you have," (2 Cor. 8:11, NLT) so that "...when we take your gifts to those who need them, they will break out in thanksgiving to God." (2 Cor. 9:11 NLT)

## What Is Hunters For The Hungry?

Established as a cooperative effort by members of the hunting community, the *Hunters for the Hungry* movement brings together hunters, sporting associations, meat processors, state meat inspectors and hunger relief organizations to help feed America's hungry. In the past few years, sportsmen nationwide have donated hundreds of thousands of pounds of venison to homeless shelters, soup kitchens and food banks. According to the Illinois Department of Natural Resources, from the 1994/95 hunting season to the 1997/98 hunting season, hunters generously donated more than 38,000 pounds of venison to food charity organizations through the *Illinois Sportsmen Against Hunger* program.

Organizations such as The NRA, Safari Club, Buckmasters, Whitetails Unlimited as well as a variety of state and local organizations assist in supporting the *Hunters for the Hungry* programs. However, despite having the support and financial backing of such well-established hunting industries and organizations, these programs would not survive and continue to distribute ground venison to families in need were it not for the generous public support from folks like you.

## How Can I Get Involved?

Donate your surplus deer harvest. If you end up with more deer than your family can possibly consume in one year, consider donating your extra game to the program. Or, even if after reading my compelling reasons to reconsider venison, you still can't bring yourself to eat it, please consider donating all or a portion of your deer.

In a recent conversation with my husband's hometown meat processor, I discovered that they processed 30,000 pounds of venison sausage last deer season. That's a heck of a load of sausage for a sparsely populated rural county. This tells me that there are a lot of folks out there who may have more venison on their hands than they know what to do with. It would be wonderful if some of that meat was donated to food banks. The good news is that processing venison into ground burger isn't near as costly as processing it all into sausage. Oh, and don't forget, it's tax deductible.

Most of the *Hunters for the Hungry* programs are not-for-profit organizations. Though many are regulated by governmental agencies, they are not state-funded programs. All of these programs generally rely solely on the generosity of hunters and other private contributors to pay for processing costs. Ideally, when a hunter presents a deer carcass to a meat processor for the *Hunters for the Hungry* program, nothing more should be required of the hunter. However, if the local program is not sufficiently funded, the hunter may be asked to pay a small processing fee or their contribution may have to be declined. Please bear in mind that many meat processors who participate in these programs are already generously donating a portion of their service fee to further the cause.

If you are like our family and you manage to productively use every scrap of venison you harvest, you could consider donating about $35 (the cost of processing one deer) to your local organization. All monetary donations to these not-for-profit programs are tax deductible if they are an IRS 501 (c) 3 approved organization.

You can be assured your payment will be tax deductible by writing the check directly to the local not-for-profit organization that administers the program. The meat processor can usually forward the check to the program administrator for reimbursement. For tax documentation purposes, you may also want a receipt.

If you or your spouse are a member of a local hunting club, archery club, sportsmen's club, shooting range, etc., spread the word about these programs during hunting season by posting information at your club, including information in your club newsletter, or by submitting information to your local press. You could also encourage your club or organization to make a yearly contribution to your local *Hunters for the Hungry* program or hold a fund-raiser. Again, be sure to notify the local press. One such effort was a Celebrity Upland Game Hunt, featuring two St. Louis Rams football players. It was hosted by the *Illinois Sportsmen Against Hunger* and netted a handsome amount.

## Who Decides What Charities Receive The Donated Venison?

This varies, depending on the particular organization that administers your state program. Although the *Illinois Sportsmen Against Hunger* and the Illinois Department of Natural Resources provide lists of food charities, food banks and food kitchens to all participating meat processors, they allow the meat processors to distribute donated ground venison to any local food charity. Since all meat processors participating in the *ISAH* program are required to clearly document deliveries of donated venison to charities, the group has a full accounting of where the donated venison is sent. If the program in your state allows it, feel free to tell the meat processor which local charity should receive your donated venison. If you know of any food banks, food pantries or food kitchens that could use ground venison, and don't currently receive any, pass along information about your local program so they can get involved.

## What If I Already Have Surplus Venison In My Freezer That I Don't Plan To Use?

According to the Illinois Department of Natural Resources, the *Illinois Sportsmen Against Hunger* program does not accept donations of processed meat directly from the hunter. However, food pantries in Illinois can accept donated venison that's been processed by a state-licensed meat processor. If you processed the venison yourself or if your processor is not state-licensed, by law, the food bank is not allowed to accept the meat.

To obtain more information on how you can get involved in the *Hunters for the Hungry, Sportsmen Against Hunger, Buckmasters Project Venison* or other similar programs in your state, check out the list that appears below.

**National**
National Rifle Association
Hunters for the Hungry
John Bailey
800-492-HUNT
email: contact@nra.org

## Alabama
Buckmasters
Project Venison
Charlie Lane
800-240-3337
email: dthornberry@buckmasters.com

## Alaska
Food Bank of Alaska - Anchorage
Alaskan Hunters Fighting Hunger
Jack Doyle
907-272-3663
email: jrdoyle@secondharvest.org

Fairbanks Community Food Bank
 Service
Hunters for the Hungry
Samantha Kirstein
907-457-4273
email: foodbank@polarnet.com

## Arizona
Phoenix Sportsmen Against Hunger
Steve Lasky
602-233-0071

## California
Orange County Sportsmen Against
 Hunger
Neal Davison
714-642-0433

Redding Sportsmen Against Hunger
Greg Morton
916-529-4284

San Francisco Bay Sportsmen Against
 Hunger
Dean Miller
415-595-5530

## Colorado
Food Bank of the Rockies
303-371-9250

## Connecticut
New England Sportsmen Against
 Hunger
C. Geoffrey Hemmenway
508-772-7000

Connecticut Hunters for the Hungry
Bobby Blackmore
860-749-0852

## Delaware
Delaware Sportsmen Against Hunger
Lloyd Alexander
302-739-5297

Buckmasters
Project Venison
Charlie Lane
800-240-3337
email: dthornberry@buckmasters.com

## Florida
Sportsmen Against Hunger
E.W. (Ted) Mayhew
904-287-0266

## Georgia
Georgia Wildlife Federation
Georgia Hunters for the Hungry
Jerry McCollum
770-929-3350

Buckmasters
Project Venison
Charlie Lane
800-240-3337
email: dthornberry@buckmasters.com

Department of Natural Resources
404-918-6400

**Illinois**
Illinois Department of Natural Resources

Illinois Sportsmen Against Hunger
Ms. Noel Laurent
217-785-5091 or 800-221-6229
email: nlaurent@dnrmail.state.il.us

Buckmasters
Project Venison
Charlie Lane
800-240-3337
email: dthornberry@buckmasters.com

**Indiana**
Indiana Deer Hunters Association
Joe Heath

**Iowa**
Iowa Department of Natural Resources
515-281-5145

**Kansas**
Kansas Department of Wildlife and Parks
316-755-2711

**Kentucky**
Hunters for the Hungry
Mike Ohlman
502-448-1309

**Louisiana**
Louisiana Department of Fish and Wildlife
504-765-2344

**Maine**
Joseph Shorthill
207-324-8070
New England Sportsmen Against Hunger
C. Geoffrey Hemmenway
508-772-7000

**Maryland**
Maryland Deer Hunters Association
Alan Ellis
410-922-5549

**Massachusetts**
New England Sportsmen Against Hunger
C. Geoffrey Hemmenway
508-772-7000

**Michigan**
Sportsmen Against Hunger
John Dickman
313-278-3663 or 616-731-3337
email:razorhead@ad.com

**Minnesota**
Minnesota Deer Hunters Association
Tony Bauer
800-450-3337

**Mississippi**
Mississippi Sportsmen Against Hunger
Hunters for the Hungry
T. Logan Russel
800-777-5001
email: roi@teclink.net

Buckmasters
Project Venison
Charlie Lane
800-240-3337
email: dthornberry@buckmasters.com

**Missouri**
Charitable Meat Donation Program
Dave Beffa
314-761-4115, Ext. 819

MDC/Bass Pro Shops
Share The Harvest
Larry Whiteley
417-832-1998

**Montana**
Sportsmen Against Hunger
Ron Barker
406-248-5553

**Nebraska**
Hunters Feeding the Hungry
Kevin Markt
402-492-9203
email: kmarkt@mitec.net

**New Hampshire**
New Hampshire Fish and Game
 Department
603-669-9725

**New Jersey**
United Bowhunters of New Jersey
Mike Volpe
609-625-4468

**New York**
New York State Conservation Council
315-894-3302

Sportsmen Against Hunger
Tom Klug
212-839-7368

Hunters Helping the Hungry
Robert Grose

Buckmasters
Project Venison
Charlie Lane
800-240-3337
email: dthornberry@buckmasters.com

**North Carolina**
Hunters for the Hungry
919-833-1923

North Carolina Department of Agricul-
 ture
Ernie Seneca
919-662-4370

Onslow County Hunters For The
 Hungry
Taking Aim Against Hunger
Myron Cross
910-455-4554
email: mdcross@onslowonline.net

**Ohio**
Hunters Helping Hand, Mercer County
Harry Sunderland
419-586-1231

Ohio Division of Wildlife
614-644-3925

Buckmasters
Project Venison
Charlie Lane
800-240-3337
email: dthornberry@buckmasters.com

Central Ohio Club of Safari Club
 International Sportsmen Against
 Hunger
Tony Gioffre
614-764-0032

**Oklahoma**
Oklahoma Wildlife Federation
Mary Dooley
405-524-7009

Sportsmen Against Hunger
Steve Scott
405-840-1980

**Oregon**
Portland Sportsmen Against Hunger

**Pennsylvania**
Hunters Sharing the Harvest
Ken Brandt
717-367-5223

Pittsburgh Sportsmen Against Hunger
Dave Baker
412-378-8474

Hunters Sharing the Harvest
814-375-4198

**Rhode Island**
New England Sportsmen Against
 Hunger
C. Geoffrey Hemmenway
508-772-7000

**South Carolina**
Hunters for the Hungry
Ted Aubert
803-783-3462

Buckmasters
Project Venison
Charlie Lane
800-240-3337
email: dthornberry@buckmasters.com

**South Dakota**
Sportsmen Against Hunger
Jeff Olson
605-342-2445

**Tennessee**
Tennessee Conservation League
Sue Garner
615-353-1133

Buckmasters
Project Venison
Charlie Lane
800-240-3337
email: dthornberry@buckmasters.com

Buckmasters One Shot Chapter Of
 East Tennessee
Project Venison - Hunters Feeding The
 Hungry
David W. Corum
423-675-1449
email: davrob@concentric.net

**Texas**
End Hunger Network
Sharon Jackson
800-992-9767

Hunters for the Hungry (Houston)
Ray Petty
713-666-7171

Awarehouse
The Joseph Project
Steve Donaldson
806-792-4007
email: stevedonaldson@door.net

Safari Club International - Dallas
Hunters for the Hungry
972-980-9800
email: biggame@intex.net

**Utah**
Utah Sportsmen Against Hunger
Bill Dodgson

**Vermont**
New England Sportsmen Against
 Hunger
C. Geoffrey Hemmenway
508-772-7000

**Virginia**
Virginia Hunters Who Care
Hunters for the Hungry
David Horne
800-352-HUNT
email: staff@4hungry.org

Ward Burton Wildlife Foundation
800-358-4608
email: Ward22Fan@aol.com

**Washington**
Sportsmen Against Hunger
Kent Klineberger
206-343-9797

Northwest Harvest
Elaine Hagglund
800-722-6924
email: nharvest@blarg.net

**West Virginia**
Hunters Helping the Hungry
Jack Cromer
304-637-0245

**Wisconsin**
Sportsmen Against Hunger
Tom Blank
414-421-7890

Buckmasters
Project Venison
Charlie Lane
800-240-3337
email: dthornberry@buckmasters.com

**Wyoming**
Sportsmen Against Hunger
Herbert Hazen
307-733-1530

Cindy Pfisterer
307-856-6603

**Canada**
Alberta Fish and Game Association
Alberta Hunters Who Care
Ron Houser - Exec VP
403-437-2342
email: avb@afga.org

## What You Should Know About Donating Deer Carcasses

When donating wild game to charitable organizations, it is important to properly handle the carcasses before processing and packaging. Wild game, when properly killed, cleaned, stored and prepared, is a wholesome and safe source of food for human consumption. Ill or diseased animals and animals from unknown sources should be condemned as unfit for human consumption and disposed of properly. Roadkill wild game is prohibited.

The following are guidelines from the Illinois Department of Natural Resources' pamphlet, *Donating Wild Game: A guide to handling and preparing wild game for charitable donations.*

## Field Dressing Carcasses

*Take care not to perforate organs in the abdominal cavity when field dressing the deer.*

1. Field dress the carcass as soon as possible after the death of the animal.

2. Perforation of the intestinal or digestive tract during field dressing, or when the deer was shot, will preclude donation due to the potential for fecal contamination of the meat.

3. Once the carcass has been field dressed and cleaned, allow air to circulate in the body cavity.

4. Cool the carcass to below 40 degrees F as quickly as possible. If the air temperature is above 40 degrees F, pack the cavity with ice and refrigerate as soon as possible.

## Evaluation Of Carcasses

1. Inspect carcass and internal organs for gross abnormalities.

2. Only healthy animals which are handled in a safe and sanitary manner may be donated as wholesome food products.

3. Deer that have been gut-shot or have evidence of unhealed old wounds will not be considered for donation.

## Transportation Of Field Dressed Carcasses

1. Do not skin the animal in the field. The skin acts as a natural protection of the meat as it is transported to the location where it will be processed. It is necessary to keep the carcasses as cool as possible during this transportation.

2. When moving the carcass in the field, place the carcass on its back and keep the exposed cavity clean.

3. At camp, home or meat processing plant, rinse out the cavity with clean, potable water.

4. Keep the carcass protected from contamination and dehydration while transporting on a clean, protected surface.

5. Take precautions to avoid contamination by chemicals such as gasoline, oil, farm chemicals, or road splash or spray.

## Holding Times And Temperatures

**Delivery of the carcasses to the meat processor should be as soon as possible.**

1. Carcasses may be hung, prior to delivery to the processing facility or charity, for no longer than 72 hours at 34 - 40 degrees F. The shortest possible hanging time is recommended to prevent potential contamination.

2. It is important to remember that when a building is not insulated, even with an outside temperature of 40 degrees F or less, the sun can cause the interior temperatures of the building to rise to 50-60 degrees F. This can result in spoilage of the meat and the growth of illness-causing bacteria. Such organisms may contaminate the carcass due to broken intestines or careless field dressing.

3. Aged wild game carcasses are not acceptable.

## Processing The Carcass

1. Keep the carcass cold, below 40 degrees F or frozen, until it is processed.

2. Any wild game, collected by individual hunters, trappers, landowners or sportsmen's organization must be processed in a state- or federally licensed and inspected facility so the processors can assess the carcasses and dispose of any that are questionable prior to distribution for human consumption.

3. When wild game carcasses are transported with other food products, they will be bagged and held in a tightly covered rigid container at temperatures less than 40 degrees F.

4. If the carcass is processed "as a service," the packaged meat must be marked with the owner's name and marked "not for sale."

# Recipes, The Moment We've All Been Waiting For

Now that you've been versed on the practical and peculiar elements of venison cookery, you're ready to roll up your sleeves, slap on your apron and whip up a tasty venison meal. Go for it! Oh, and don't forget to have fun!

## Recipe Table of Contents

## Making Sense Of Symbols

### Buck Savor Tips

Handy, dandy little time-saving, money-pinching, savory tips. Some are mini-versions of ideas and suggestions described in Chapter 5, Tips, Tricks and Tools of the Trade. Others are new revelations as they came to me while cooking or testing the recipe.

### Bull's Eye Recipe

All of my recipes endured the scrutiny of my entire family. These recipes rated so high, we decided to call them "Bull's Eye Recipes." One of the qualifying criteria is that my husband would be willing to take it to work to feed 'the gang.'

### Kid Friendly

Fairly self-explanatory, this symbol implies that kids usually wolf these dishes down in a flash. No wrinkly noses. The finicky yet fair judge was my 7-year-old daughter. Since my 2-year-old pretty much eats anything set in front of her, I decided she wasn't a very impartial judge.

If you don't see a symbol next to a recipe, keep in mind that the above rating system is very reflective of the judges' (my husband and eldest daughter) personal styles. Many of my personal favorites are not highlighted. The Helregel family consensus is that they are all quite good. And, in case you are wondering, yes, I did have some failures. They didn't make it into this book.

# Recipes ———————————————

## Appetizers

### BBQ Meatballs

1 pound ground venison
1/2 cup dry bread crumbs
1/3 cup onion, minced
1/4 cup milk
1 egg, beaten
1 tablespoon dried parsley
1/2 teaspoon salt
1/2 teaspoon celery salt
1/4 teaspoon pepper
1 ½ teaspoons Worcestershire sauce
<u>Sauce</u>
1 bottle (12 ounces) chili sauce
1 jar (10 ounces) grape jelly

In a mixing bowl, combine the first 10 ingredients and mix well. Shape into 1-inch balls. Place on ungreased baking sheets. Bake at 450 degrees for 10 minutes, turning once at 7 or 8 minutes. Meanwhile, for sauce, combine chili sauce and jelly in a large saucepan or Dutch oven. Heat over medium heat, stirring constantly, until jelly has melted. Add baked meatballs and heat through. Serve warm in a crock pot set on Low, or in an appropriate server. Makes about 4 to 5 dozen.

# Cocktail Meatballs

2 pounds ground venison
2 eggs, beaten
1 ¼ cup dry bread crumbs
1/2 cup milk
1/2 teaspoon salt
1/2 teaspoon celery salt
1/2 teaspoon garlic salt
1/2 teaspoon onion powder
1/2 teaspoon pepper

Sauce
1 can (28 ounces) diced tomatoes with liquid
1/2 cup packed brown sugar
1/4 cup vinegar
1/2 teaspoon salt
1 ½ teaspoons onion, finely chopped
10 gingersnaps, finely crushed

Place first 9 ingredients in large mixing bowl and mix well. Shape into 1 to
1 ¼-inch balls. Place on ungreased baking sheets. Bake at 450 degrees for
10 minutes, turning once at 7 or 8 minutes. Meanwhile, for sauce, combine
tomatoes, brown sugar, vinegar, salt and onion in large saucepan or Dutch
oven. Bring to a boil. Add gingersnaps and mix well. Continue boiling until
sauce is thick and clear. Reduce heat to simmer and add meatballs. Heat
through. Serve warm in a crock pot set on LOW or in an appropriate serving
dish. Makes about 5 to 6 dozen.

## Crescent Party Triangles

4 ounces cream cheese, softened (1/2 of an 8 ounce package)
1/2 egg, beaten (discard other 1/2)
1/4 teaspoon garlic puree
2 tablespoons Parmesan/Romano cheese
1/2 pound ground venison
1/2 can (5 ounces) sliced water chestnuts, chopped
1/2 can (4 ounces) sliced mushrooms, chopped
1/2 teaspoon garlic salt or garlic puree
1/4 teaspoon celery salt
2 teaspoons onion, minced
3 tablespoons beef broth
2 or 3 packages (8 ounces, each) refrigerator crescent rolls

Dipping Sauce
1/2 cup sour cream
1 teaspoon horseradish sauce

Combine first 4 ingredients and blend well. Set aside. In a skillet over medium heat, combine ground venison, chestnuts, mushrooms, garlic salt (or puree), celery salt, onion and broth. Cook until venison is crumbled and done. Coat a cookie sheet or baking stone with non-stick cooking spray. Place a crescent triangle on the cookie sheet. Spread it with cream cheese mixture to 1/8 inch of the edge. Spoon about 1 tablespoon of meat mixture on top of cream cheese spread. Cover with another crescent triangle and seal the edges by crimping with a fork. Repeat until all ingredients have been exhausted. Bake triangles at 375 degrees for 15-18 minutes or until crescent pastry is golden brown. Combine sour cream and horseradish sauce. Serve with warm triangles. This recipe can be easily doubled for a larger batch. Makes 8 – 12.

 These crescent triangles also serve well for breakfast or a brunch.

## Buck Eyes

1/2 cup soy sauce (scant)
1/3 cup vegetable oil
1/4 cup lemon juice
1/8 cup Worcestershire sauce
1/8 cup prepared mustard
2 tablespoons onion, minced
1 ½ to 2 pounds venison round steak, cut into thin strips
3 or 4 cans (8 ounces, each) whole chestnuts, drained and rinsed
2 pounds sliced hickory smoked bacon

Combine first 6 ingredients. Mix well. Add venison steak strips. Coat steak strips well with marinade. Cover and marinade in refrigerator for at least 2 - 4 hours. Cut slab(s) of bacon in half. To assemble Buck Eyes, take 1/2 strip of bacon and lay it on a cutting board. Lay a marinated strip of meat in the center of the bacon strip. Put a chestnut in the center, on top of the steak strip. Wrap one end of bacon over chestnut and continue to roll. Pierce all with a toothpick. Repeat until all Buck Eyes are done. Place Buck Eyes on a broiler pan to allow fat and juices to drain without creating a fire in your oven (trust me, this has happened). Broil on 2nd rack from the top for 10-15 minutes or until meat is cooked through and bacon appears slightly crunchy or charred. You may want to turn them over once halfway through the cooking time. If necessary, drain Buck Eyes on a paper towel before serving. Makes about 4 to 5 dozen.

## Barnyard Barbecue Barrels

1 tube (10 ounces) refrigerated buttermilk biscuits
1/2 to 3/4 pound ground venison
1/4 cup onion, minced
1 teaspoon celery salt
1/2 cup ketchup
3 tablespoons brown sugar
1 tablespoon cider vinegar
1/2 teaspoon chili powder
1 cup fancy shredded cheddar cheese

Separate dough into 10 biscuits. Flatten into 5-inch circles with the bottom of a dry measuring cup. Press each biscuit into the bottom and up the sides of a greased muffin cup. Set aside. In a skillet over medium heat, combine ground venison, onion and celery salt. Cook until venison is crumbled and done. In a small bowl, mix ketchup, brown sugar, vinegar and chili powder. Stir until smooth. Add to meat and mix well. Fill each muffin cup with meat mixture and sprinkle with cheese. Bake at 375 degrees for approximately 12-15 minutes or until golden brown. Let stand for 5 minutes before removing from tin and serving. Makes 10.

 These little barrels are also a big hit with the kiddies for lunch.

## Miniature Teriyaki Kabobs

1 pound venison round steak, cut into long, thin strips (about 3 to 4 inches long)
1 can (11 ounces) mandarin oranges
1/4 cup teriyaki sauce
1 tablespoon honey
1 tablespoon vinegar
1/8 teaspoon garlic powder
16 to 20 bamboo skewers (6- or 8-inch)

In a small bowl, combine teriyaki sauce, honey, vinegar and garlic powder. Add venison steak strips and marinate for at least 4 hours or overnight. Soak bamboo skewers in water for 10 minutes. Thread venison steak strips, accordion style, with mandarin oranges on skewers. Grill kabobs for approximately 10 minutes, or until meat is cooked through. Turn kabobs and brush with sauce at least once while grilling. Or, place kabobs on broiler pan and brush with sauce. Broil, 6 inches from heat, approximately 10-15 minutes or until meat is cooked through. Turn kabobs and brush with sauce at least once while broiling. Makes 16 to 20 appetizers.

## Sausage Stuffed Mushrooms

1/2  pound ground venison
1/2 teaspoon celery salt
1/2 teaspoon ground sage
1/4 teaspoon ground coriander
1/4 teaspoon dried marjoram
1/4 teaspoon black pepper (optional for spicier sausage)
2 packages (8 ounces, each) fresh medium mushrooms
3/4 cup shredded mozzarella cheese
1/4 cup dry bread crumbs
1 tablespoon dried parsley

In a bowl, combine ground venison with celery salt, sage, coriander, marjoram and black pepper, if desired. Mix well. Remove stems from mushroom caps and set caps aside. Finely chop mushroom stems in a mini-chopper. In a skillet, combine meat mixture and stems. Cook over medium heat until meat is cooked through and the mushroom stems have released their juices. Remove from heat. Stir in cheese, bread crumbs and parsley. With your fingers, scoop the meat mixture into each mushroom cap. Place mushroom caps on a jelly roll pan or cookie sheet. Bake at 450 degrees F for about 8 minutes. Makes about 3 dozen.

Make lots of room in those mushrooms for the stuffing! Use a tomato corer to scrape out the caps after you have removed the stems.

For a milder tasting appetizer, omit the sage, coriander, marjoram and black pepper. Substitute 2 tablespoons of minced onion and 1/2 teaspoon celery salt.

## Venison Egg Rolls

1/2 pound ground venison
2 teaspoons celery, finely chopped
2 teaspoons onion, finely chopped
2 cups shredded green cabbage
1/2 cup sliced water chestnuts, drained and finely chopped
1/3 cup shredded carrot
1/8 teaspoon ground ginger
1 tablespoon cornstarch
1 tablespoon dry cooking sherry
1 tablespoon soy sauce
1 tablespoon sesame oil
14 to 16 egg roll skins (7-inch square)
1 egg yolk mixed with 1 teaspoon water
3 cups cooking oil
sweet and sour sauce or hot mustard

In a skillet over medium heat, combine ground venison, celery, and onion. Cook until venison is crumbled and done. Combine meat mixture, cabbage, chestnuts, carrot, ginger, cornstarch, sherry, soy sauce and sesame oil. Toss and mix well. Place 2 heaping tablespoons of egg roll mixture in center of egg roll skin. Dab or brush all four corners of skin with egg mixture. Bring bottom corner over meat and tuck under meat. Fold both side corners in and roll up. Make sure last corner sticks. In a medium size, non-stick saucepan, heat oil over medium-high heat (but not too hot). Or, use a deep fat fryer. When oil is hot enough, use tongs to lower egg roll into oil. Cook 3 egg rolls at a time for about 2 to 2 ½ minutes, or until golden brown, turning over once. Remove from oil and drain on a paper towel lined plate. Serve with sweet and sour sauce or hot mustard, if desired. Makes 14 to 16 egg rolls.

How do you know when the oil is hot enough? Take a small piece of egg roll or wonton pastry and drop it into the oil.

- If it does not sizzle at all, it is not hot enough. Wait a little longer or turn up the heat.
- If it sizzles and looks golden brown after about 2 minutes, it's just the right temperature. Start cooking. There is probably no need to adjust the heat.
- If it sizzles and immediately becomes dark brown or turns dark brown after about 2 minutes, it is too hot. Turn down the heat a notch or two.

## Crispy Venison Wontons

1/2 pound ground venison
2 teaspoons onion, finely chopped
2 tablespoons finely chopped water chestnuts
1/4 cup green onions and tops, finely chopped
1 tablespoon soy sauce
1 teaspoon cornstarch
1/8 teaspoon ground ginger
24 to 36 wonton skins
1 egg mixed with 1 teaspoon water
3 cups cooking oil
sweet and sour sauce and/or hot mustard

In a bowl, combine ground venison, chestnuts, green onions, soy sauce, cornstarch and ginger. Mix and blend well. Place 1 heaping teaspoon of meat mixture in center of each wonton skin. Brush edges of wonton skin with egg mixture. Fold wonton skin in 1/2, forming a triangle. Bring both side corners together and overlap. Press together to seal. In a medium size, non-stick saucepan, heat oil over medium-high heat (but not too hot!). When oil is hot enough, use tongs to lower wontons into oil. Cook about 6 or 7 at a time for 2 minutes each, or until golden brown, turning over once. Remove from oil and drain on a paper towel lined plate. Serve with sweet and sour sauce or hot mustard, if desired. Makes about 2 to 3 dozen.

## Mexican Wontons

1/2 pound ground venison
1/2 onion, finely chopped
3 tablespoons thick 'n chunky salsa (of preferred heat level)
1 teaspoon minced garlic
1/2 teaspoon ground sage
1/2 teaspoon ground cumin
1 can (4 ounces) chopped green chilies
1 ½ cups shredded Monterey Jack cheese
24-36 wonton skins
1 egg mixed with 1 teaspoon water
3 cups cooking oil
additional salsa, ranch dressing and/or sour cream

In a skillet over medium heat, combine ground venison, onion, salsa, garlic, sage and cumin. Cook until venison is crumbled and done. Set aside. Brush all edges of wonton skins with egg yolk mixture. Place 1/8 teaspoon green chilies in center of wonton. Add 1 heaping teaspoon of meat mixture and top with 1 teaspoon shredded cheese. Bring all four corners of wonton skin together to a point and seal edges. In a medium size, non-stick saucepan, heat oil over medium-high heat (but not too hot!). When oil is hot enough, use tongs to lower wontons into oil. Cook about 6 or 7 at a time for 2 minutes each, or until golden brown, turning over once. Remove from oil and drain on a paper towel lined plate. Serve with additional salsa, sour cream or ranch dressing. Makes about 2 to 3 dozen.

## Con Queso Dip

1/2 pound ground venison
1 pound (16 ounces) pasteurized process cheese loaf with jalpeño peppers,
 cut into cubes
1 cup chopped, seeded tomato
1 can (4 ounces) chopped green chilies, drained
1/4 cup chopped ripe black olives

In a skillet over medium heat, combine ground venison, tomatoes and chilies. Cook until venison is crumbled and done. Drain and reserve juices from meat mixture. In a non-stick saucepan over low- to medium heat, melt the cheese. Once melted, add meat mixture and black olives. Add reserved juice, as needed, to bring dip to desired consistency. Serve with tortilla chips or use as a baked potato topper. Makes about 3 cups.

## Cranberry Meatballs

1 pound ground venison
1/2 cup corn flake crumbs
1 egg, beaten
1 tablespoon dried parsley
1 tablespoon soy sauce
1/4 teaspoon garlic powder
1/8 teaspoon black pepper

Sauce
1 can (16 ounces) whole-berry cranberry sauce
1 bottle (12 ounces) chili sauce
1/3 cup catsup
2 tablespoons packed brown sugar
1 tablespoon lemon juice
2 teaspoons minced onion (fresh or dried)

In a bowl, combine ground venison, corn flake crumbs, egg, soy sauce, garlic powder and pepper. Mix well. Shape into 1-inch balls. Place meatballs on a cookie sheet and bake at 450 degrees F for about 10 minutes, turning once at 7 or 8 minutes. Meanwhile, in saucepan over medium heat, combine all sauce ingredients. Add cooked meatballs and simmer until heated through. Serve warm in a crock pot set on Low, or in an appropriate server. Makes about 2 dozen.

 The sauce recipe is actually enough for two batches of meatballs. Double the meatball ingredients and you'll have about twice the fixin's.

# Burgers And Meatloaf

## Marinated Venison Burgers

3/4 cup soy sauce
2/3 cup vegetable oil
1/2 cup lemon juice
1/4 cup Worcestershire sauce
1/4 cup prepared mustard
1/2 cup onion, or finely chopped
1 pound ground venison

Form ground venison into generous patties, not too thin, but not too large around as they won't shrink very much. Place patties in a glass baking dish and set aside. Combine all other ingredients and blend well. Pour marinade over the patties. Cover and refrigerate for at least one hour (preferably two or more), turning the patties over at least once during that time. Grill or broil the patties for about 5 to 10 minutes or until patties are cooked through. Serve. This recipe makes an enormous amount of marinade. I usually make 1/2 a batch if I am grilling only 4 or 5 patties. This also makes a great marinade for venison tenderloins and boneless chicken breasts! Makes 4 or 5 burgers using 1 pound of ground venison.

## Golden Venison Meatloaf

1 pound ground venison
1 can (10 ¾ ounces) Campbell's Golden Mushroom soup, divided
1/2 cup dry bread crumbs or cracker crumbs
1/2 cup onion, finely chopped
1/3 cup celery, finely chopped (or use 1 teaspoon celery salt)
1 tablespoon Worcestershire sauce
1 egg beaten
dash black pepper

In a bowl, thoroughly mix ground venison, 3/4 can soup, crumbs, onion, celery, Worcestershire, egg and pepper. Pour mixture into a glass baking dish or glass pie plate and gently shape into an oblong form about 1 to 1 ½-inch high loaf. It will not be a firm loaf, it may look runny but that is okay. Spread the remaining soup on top of the meatloaf. Cover dish with foil and bake at 350 degrees for 1 hour or until done. The soup creates a "gravy" that you can scoop out with a spoon and tastes great on mashed potatoes. Serves 4 – 6.

 I use to despise recipes that called for bread crumbs….mostly because about the only "crumbs" that existed in my house were the ones that ended up in my dustpan after I swept the kitchen floor. Here's a great way to make sure you have plenty of dried bread crumbs handy for awhile.

1. Buy the cheapest loaf (or two) of white bread you can find.

2. Take out all your frustration for the week and tear each slice of bread into chunks.

3. Place the chunks in a very large bowl or lay them on a couple of cookie sheets. They will dry out faster if allowed to dry on cookie sheets or on some paper towels in a vacant countertop.

4. Let them sit for a day. Stir. Let them sit another day. Stir. Keep doing this until your bread chunks turn as about as hard as croutons.

5. Place as many dried chunks of bread in a sturdy air tight storage bag. Seal.

6. Take out some more frustration and crush those chunks with your rolling pin. Continue until all the chunks have turned to crumbs. If some remaining chunks are still a little moist, give them another day or two before you crush them.

7. Store your bread crumbs in a sealed storage bag in the freezer. They keep forever.

 Fresh out of bread crumbs? Crush some unsalted (or salted, if desperate) crackers, oyster crackers or soup crackers. Crushed unseasoned croutons work well too.

## Mock Filet Mignon

3/4 pound ground venison
1 cup cooked rice
1/2 cup onion, minced
1/8 teaspoon garlic powder
1/8 teaspoon celery salt
1/2 teaspoon salt
dash of pepper
2 tablespoons Worcestershire sauce
5 to 8 strips hickory smoked bacon

In a mixing bowl, combine ground venison, rice, onion, garlic powder, celery salt, salt, pepper and Worcestershire sauce. Mix thoroughly with a fork. Shape into round patties. Wrap entire strip of bacon around each patty (bacon may overlap some). Secure with a wooden toothpick, if necessary. Place mock filets in an ungreased, shallow, glass baking dish. Bake at 450 degrees for 20 minutes or to desired doneness, turning once 1/2 way through cooking time. Makes approximately 4 – 5 patties.

## Venison Chili Burgers

1 pound ground venison
1/2 cup canned kidney beans, rinsed and drained
1/2 cup frozen corn kernels, thawed
1 cup chili sauce, divided
2 tablespoons plain dried bread crumbs
1 egg white
2 teaspoons chili powder
3/4 teaspoon ground cumin
1/2 teaspoon dried oregano
1/2 teaspoon celery salt

Chop kidney beans in a mini-chopper or by hand. In a bowl, combine ground venison, chopped kidney beans, corn, 1/2 cup of the chili sauce, bread crumbs, egg white, chili powder, cumin, oregano and celery salt. By hand or with a potato masher, mix well to combine all ingredients. Shape into 4 or 5 patties (they are somewhat fragile so keep them hearty). Grill or broil the burgers for about 5-10 minutes or until cooked through. Top the burgers with remaining chili sauce (if desired) and serve on a bun. Serves 4 – 5.

 Forgot to pull out your frozen veggies to defrost them? Zap them for about 30 seconds on HIGH in the microwave. Don't worry if they appear to be a bit cooked. We won't tell anybody.

## Hot 'n Spicy Venison Burgers

1 pound ground venison
1 egg white
3 tablespoons onion, minced
2 teaspoons Worcestershire sauce
2 teaspoons prepared hot mustard (or sweet/hot)
1 teaspoon minced garlic
1/4 teaspoon black pepper
1/2 teaspoon cayenne pepper

In a bowl, combine all ingredients and mix well by hand or with a potato masher. Shape into 4 or 5 round patties. Grill or broil burgers for about 5-10 minutes or until cooked through. Serve on a bun with your favorite toppings. If you prefer a milder taste, reduce amount of cayenne pepper. Serves 4 – 5.

## Herb and Cheese Stuffed Venison Burgers

1/4 cup shredded cheddar cheese
2 tablespoons cream cheese or reduced-fat cream cheese
1 tablespoon dried parsley
1 teaspoon Dijon mustard

1 pound ground venison
2 green onions, thinly sliced
2 tablespoons dried bread crumbs
2 tablespoons ketchup
2 teaspoons Dijon mustard
1/2 teaspoon celery salt
1/2 teaspoon dried rosemary
1/4 teaspoon dried sage

In a small bowl, combine cheddar cheese, cream cheese, parsley and 1 teaspoon of the mustard. Set aside. In a separate bowl, combine ground venison, onions, bread crumbs, ketchup, celery salt, rosemary, sage, and remaining mustard. Mix well by hand or with a potato masher. Shape mixture into 4 or 5 balls. Divide reserved cheese mixture into 4ths or 5ths (depending on the number of burgers). Holding a ball of ground meat, push your thumb into the center of the ball. Place a ball of cheese mixture into this center well and pull the meat over the cheese to seal. Now, gently shape the ball into a patty. Grill or broil the burgers for approximately 5-10 minutes or until cooked through. Serve on a bun. Serves 4 – 5.

 It's a venison burger, not a work of art. Don't spend anymore than about 30 seconds forming each patty and don't sweat it if they don't look like perfect little moon pies. Also, don't wig out when the filling oozes out a bit while you are grilling these scrumptious, mouth watering burgers.

## Cheese Filled Venison Loaf

1 pound ground venison
1/2 cup dry bread crumbs
1 egg
1/4 cup barbecue sauce
1/2 teaspoon celery salt
1/4 teaspoon black pepper
1 cup shredded cheddar cheese
1/4 cup green onions, sliced
additional barbecue sauce

In a medium mixing bowl, combine ground venison, bread crumbs, egg, barbecue sauce, celery salt and pepper. On a sheet of wax paper, shape meat mixture into 14-inch x 8-inch rectangle. Sprinkle cheese and onions evenly over meat mixture to within 1 inch of edges. Starting with the short side, tightly roll up the meat, peeling back wax paper while rolling. Discard wax paper. Pinch ends and seam of roll to seal. Place meat roll with seam-side-down in a baking dish and cover with foil. Bake at 350 degrees F for 1 to 1/2 hours or until meat is firm and cooked through. Drain off any juices and brush barbecue sauce evenly over meat roll. Bake for an additional 10 minutes. Let stand for 10 minutes before slicing. Slice and serve on hamburger buns. Serves 4 – 6.

 This "burger" has lots of potential. Feel free to add any of your favorite "toppings", such as real bacon bits, chopped mushrooms, etc., to the filling.

## Po' Boy's Pot Roast

1 pound ground venison
1 can (5 ounces) evaporated milk
1/4 cup ketchup
1/2 cup dry bread crumbs
1 tablespoon Worcestershire sauce
3/4 teaspoon ground cumin
1/4 teaspoon celery salt
1/8 teaspoon black pepper
1 can (14 ounces) beef broth
4 small onions, peeled and quartered
2 cans (15 ounces, each) whole potatoes, drained
or 8 small potatoes, peeled and quartered
1 ½ to 2 cups baby carrots (fresh or frozen)
1 large green pepper, cut into strips (optional)
1 ½ tablespoons dried parsley

In a large bowl, combine milk, ketchup, bread crumbs, Worcestershire
sauce, cumin, salt and pepper. Add ground venison and mix well. Shape
meat mixture into an oblong meat loaf and place in a 13-inch x 9-inch
baking dish. Place onions, potatoes, carrots and green pepper around the
loaf. Pour broth over vegetables and meat loaf. Sprinkle all with parsley.
Cover with foil and bake at 350 degrees F for 1 to 1 ½ hours or until meat is
cooked through and vegetables are tender. Serves 6 – 8.

## Venison Meat Muffins

1 pound ground venison
3/4 cup creamed corn
1/3 cup ketchup
1 ½ tablespoons Worcestershire Sauce
1/2 cup dried bread crumbs
1/2 teaspoon cumin
1 teaspoon chili powder

Topping Sauce
1/2 cup packed brown sugar
1/3 cup ketchup parsley

In a bowl, combine all ingredients except those for the sauce. Mix well.
Divide venison mixture into 9 equal portions. Pat portions lightly into 2 1/2-inch muffin cups and place in muffin pan. Bake at 350 degrees F for 25 minutes. Meanwhile, mix topping and set aside. After muffins have baked for 25 minutes, brush or spoon topping over each meat muffin. Bake an additional 10 minutes or until meat is cooked through. Let stand a few minutes before removing from pan. Makes 9 meat muffins.

 If you don't want to use muffin cups or liners, generously grease or butter a muffin pan. You may still have to work a little to get them out, but they will taste good.

# Casseroles

### Tater Puff Casserole

1 pound ground venison
2/3 cup, finely or coarsely chopped onion
1/3 cup celery, finely chopped (or use 1 teaspoon celery salt)
1 can (10 ½ ounces) cream of chicken soup
6-8 slices of American or Velveeta brand cheese
frozen tater puffs

In a skillet over medium heat, combine ground venison, onion and celery.
Cook until venison is crumbled and done. Spread meat evenly in the bottom
a glass baking dish. Spread soup over meat. Place slices of cheese over layer
of soup. Top with a single layer of tater puffs. Bake uncovered at 375
degrees for 45 minutes. Serves 4 – 6.

 This dish makes for great leftovers, as it re-heats quite well in the
microwave oven.

### Baked Spaghetti

1 pound ground venison
1/3 cup celery, finely chopped (or use 1 teaspoon celery salt)
1/2 cup onion, finely chopped
1 ½ teaspoons minced garlic (or 1 teaspoon garlic puree)
1 jar (26 ounces) CLASSICO Tomato and Basil Spaghetti Sauce (or your
favorite brand)
2 cups shredded cheddar cheese
1/2 cup Parmesan cheese
16-20 ounces cooked spaghetti noodles

In a skillet over medium heat, combine ground venison, celery, onion and garlic. Cook until venison is crumbled and done. Spray glass casserole dish with non-stick cooking spray. Layer 1/2 noodles, 1/2 sauce and sprinkle with shredded cheddar and Parmesan cheese. Repeat. Bake uncovered at 350 degrees for 1/2 hour or until cheese is slightly golden/brown. Serves 4 – 6.


## Wild Rice and Mushroom Casserole

1 can (14 ½ ounces) beef broth
1 cup water
1/3 cup wild rice, rinsed and drained
1 pound ground venison
1 cup celery, finely chopped
1/2 cup onion, chopped
1 cup sliced fresh mushrooms
1/2 teaspoon minced garlic
1 (10 ¾-ounce) can condensed cream of mushroom soup
1/2 cup uncooked long grain rice
1/8 teaspoon black pepper

In a medium saucepan, bring broth and water to boil. Remove from heat and add wild rice. Cover and let stand. In a skillet over medium heat, combine ground venison, celery, onion, mushrooms and garlic. Cook until venison is crumbled and done. Add soup, long grain rice and black pepper to meat mixture and mix well. In a 2 quart baking dish, combine meat mixture with wild rice mixture and broth. Mix well. Cover and bake at 350 degrees F for 1 hour or until rice is cooked through. Makes 8 servings.

## Whitetail Lasagna

1 pound ground venison (or less)
1/3 cup celery, finely chopped (or use 1 teaspoon celery salt)
1/2 cup onion, finely chopped
1 ½ teaspoons minced garlic (or 1 teaspoon garlic puree)
1 ½ jars (26 ounces, each) CLASSICO Tomato and Basil Spaghetti Sauce
 (or your favorite kind)
12 lasagna noodles cooked
1/2 to 3/4 cup of grated Parmesan cheese (I prefer Sargento or Kraft fresh-
grated)

Ricotta Mixture
1 ½ containers (16 ounces, each) ricotta cheese (about 22 ounces total)
4 ½ tablespoons grated Parmesan (I prefer Sargento or Kraft fresh-grated)
3 tablespoons parsley flakes
2 eggs, beaten
1 teaspoon salt

In a skillet over medium heat, combine ground venison, celery, onion and
garlic. Cook until venison is crumbled and done. While boiling noodles,
combine all ingredients for the ricotta mixture and blend well. Preheat oven
to 350 degrees F. Lightly spray glass lasagna pan with non-stick spray. Place
layer of 4 lasagna noodles on bottom of dish. Spread 1/3 of sauce evenly
over noodles. Sprinkle 1/2 of meat mixture. Spread 1/2 of ricotta mixture
over meat. Add another layer of 4 lasagna noodles, 1/3 sauce, 1/2 meat
mixture and remaining 1/2 of ricotta. Add final layer of 4 lasagna noodles
and top with remaining 1/3 of sauce. Sprinkle with 1/2 to 3/4 cup of fresh
grated Parmesan cheese or a combination of Parmesan and Romano cheese.
Bake for 45 minutes or until heated through. Let stand for 10 minutes before
serving. Serves 6 – 8.

 Don't want to open a whole jar of sauce only to use 1/2 of it?
Substitute 1 ¼ cup (10 ounces) tomato puree and a dash of Italian
Seasoning for the other 1/2 jar of sauce.

Trying to figure out how you're going to *spread* a glob of ricotta mixture? I find that a cake decorator press or fluted icing bag works well to evenly 'spread' this testy layer.

## Taco Shell Casserole

1 pound ground venison
2 tablespoons onion, minced
1 teaspoon chili powder
3 ounces of cream cheese, softened
2 ½ cups medium shell macaroni, cooked and drained
1 cup prepared taco sauce
2 cups shredded taco cheese (or 1 cup each of cheddar and Monterey Jack cheese)
2 cups crushed tortilla chips
2 cups shredded lettuce
2 tomatoes, diced
sour cream
additional taco sauce

In a skillet over medium heat, combine ground venison, onion and chili powder. Cook until venison is crumbled and done. Add sour cream and heat through. Mix meat and macaroni until well combined. Pour meat and macaroni in a 13 x 9-inch casserole dish coated with cooking spray. Pour taco sauce over meat and mac mixture. Top with crushed tortilla chips. Bake at 350 degrees  F for about 15 minutes or until heated through. Remove casserole from oven and sprinkle lettuce, cheese and diced tomato. Serve with sour cream and additional taco sauce. Serves 4 – 6.

## Hearty Hunter's Pie

4 1/2 cups peeled, cubed potatoes
1 cup sour cream
2 tablespoons butter or margarine
milk
1/2 cup fresh grated Parmesan or finely shredded cheddar cheese
salt and pepper *or* garlic salt to taste
1 pound ground venison
1 cup sliced carrots (fresh or frozen)
1 cup onion, coarsely chopped or diced
1/2 cup green pepper, chopped
1/2 cup celery, finely chopped
1/2 teaspoon bottled, minced garlic
1 can (14 ½ ounces) whole tomatoes, undrained and chopped
2 teaspoons Worcestershire sauce
1 cup frozen peas
1 teaspoon dried basil
1/2 teaspoon dried oregano
1 bay leaf
2 tablespoons flour
2 tablespoons water
sliced butter or margarine
paprika

Cook potatoes in boiling water until tender. Meanwhile, in a skillet over medium heat, combine ground venison, carrots, onion, green pepper, celery and garlic. Cook until meat is done. Add tomatoes with juice, Worcestershire sauce, peas, basil, oregano and bay leaf. Simmer approximately 20 minutes. Meanwhile, drain potatoes and combine with sour cream and butter. Mash. Add milk as necessary until you obtain desired consistency. Blend in desired flavor of cheese. Season with salt and pepper or garlic salt to taste. When meat mixture is done simmering, remove and discard bay leaf. Combine flour and water. Add to meat mixture and blend well. Spoon meat into a 3-quart casserole dish coated with cooking spray. Spoon and spread potato mixture over meat. Top with slices of butter or margarine. Sprinkle with paprika. Bake uncovered at 350 degrees F for 20 to 25 minutes. Serves 6.

When mashing the potatoes, pick the flavor combination that works best for you. I tend to pair the Parmesan cheese with the garlic salt and the cheddar cheese with plain old salt and pepper.

## Baked Ziti Casserole

1 pound ground venison
1 cup onion, chopped
1 cup fresh sliced mushrooms, chopped
1 teaspoon minced garlic
1 ½ teaspoons dried parsley
1 jar (26 ounces) CLASSICO Tomato and Basil Pasta Sauce (or your favorite)
1 cup shredded cheddar cheese
3 cups cooked ziti or other tubular pasta
Parmesan cheese

Cook pasta according to package directions. While pasta is cooking, combine ground venison, onion, mushrooms, garlic and parsley in a skillet over medium heat. Cook until venison is crumbled and done. Add pasta sauce. Heat through. Combine cooked pasta and meat sauce. Mix well. Pour into a casserole dish coated with non-stick cooking spray. Sprinkle with cheese. Bake at 350 degrees F for about 15 minutes. Serve with Parmesan cheese and garlic bread.

## Venison Pot Pies

1/2 pound ground venison
1/2 cup onion, chopped
1 stalk celery, finely chopped
1/3 cup frozen carrots, defrosted and chopped
1/4 cup frozen peas
1/2 can (7 ounces) sliced mushrooms, drained and chopped
1/2 cup canned, sliced potatoes – drained and chopped
1/2 can (10 ½ ounces) beef gravy – or 2/3 cup homemade beef gravy
1 package (2 single) refrigerated pie pastries
1 tablespoon butter, melted

In a skillet over medium heat, combine ground venison, onion and celery. Cook until venison is crumbled and done. Remove from heat. Add carrots, peas, mushrooms, potatoes and beef gravy. Mix well. If mixture is hot, allow to cool a bit. Unfold pie pastries. Cut each pie pastry in half along seam. Spoon 1/4 of meat mixture onto 1/2 of each pastry. Spread to within ½ inch of the edge. Fold pastry over meat mixture and seal open edges with a fork. Place on non-stick baking sheets (or spray with non-stick cooking spray). Cut 3 slits in top of each pot pie. Brush each pot pie with melted butter. Bake at 400 degrees F for 20 to 22 minutes or until pastry is golden. Makes 4 pot pies.

# Chili, Soups and Stews

## Chili

*a simple, soupy variety that you will want to sop up with bread or crackers or grilled cheese sandwiches*

1 pound ground venison
1 cup onion, diced
1 cup green pepper, diced
1 ½ teaspoons celery salt
2 cans (28 ounces, each) diced tomatoes with juice
2 cans (30 ounces, each) red kidney beans, drained
2 to 3 tablespoons chili powder
1 can (11 ½ ounces) tomato juice (about 1 ½ cups)
oyster or soup crackers, optional
shredded cheddar cheese, optional

In a skillet over medium heat, combine ground venison, onion, green pepper and celery salt. Cook until venison is crumbled and done. Combine meat mixture, tomatoes, beans and chili powder in a crock pot or stock pot. Add tomato juice as needed to obtain desired consistency in your soup. Cook in crock pot on High (about 1-3 hours) or in stock pot over medium/high heat (about 30-45 minutes) until done. Serve with crackers and cheese. This makes a great soup for Super Bowl Sunday. Serves 6 – 8.

 If you like your chili loaded with lots of chunky onion and green pepper, by all means add more.

## Zesty Chili

*a thicker, zestier chili that is also good served with Tortillas and cheese*

1 pound ground venison
3/4 cup celery, finely or coarsely chopped
1 cup onion, finely or coarsely chopped
1 cup green pepper, chopped
1 ½ teaspoons minced garlic (or 1 teaspoon garlic puree)
1 ½ teaspoons parsley flakes
1 ½ teaspoons Worcestershire sauce
1 ½ tablespoons chili powder
1 to 1 ½ teaspoons hot pepper sauce
2 ½ cups water
1 can (29 ounces) tomato puree
1 ½ to 2 cans (16 ounces, each) dark red kidney beans, drained
2 cans (16 ounces, each) pinto beans, drained

Combine first five ingredients in a large skillet over medium heat. Cook until venison is crumbled and done. Combine the meat mixture and remaining ingredients in a crock pot or stock pot. Cook in crock pot on High (about 1-3 hours) or in stock pot over medium/high heat (about 30-45 minutes) until done. Serve with crackers, tortillas and/or cheddar cheese. I always get rave reviews on this dish – and no one ever guessed it had venison in it! Serves 6 – 8.

 Proverbs 14:1 states "*A wise woman builds her house*" (NLT). My mother-in-law, a very wise woman, always kept a supply of freshly chopped onion and freshly chopped green pepper tucked away in her freezer. This little "housekeeping or homemaking" tip has served me quite well in desperate times when I've needed to whip up something in a flash, like chili. Works well for chopped celery and dried bread crumbs too [hint, hint].

 This chili also makes for a great tortilla dip or baked potato topper so take a crock pot full along with a large bag of tortilla chips and shredded cheese to your next potluck gathering.

## Red, Black and White Bean Chili

1 pound ground venison
1 teaspoon celery salt
1 teaspoon ground sage
1/2 teaspoon ground coriander
1/2 teaspoon dried marjoram
1 cup onion, cut into 1/2-inch pieces
1 cup sweet red pepper, cut into 1/2-inch pieces
1 cup green pepper, cut into 1/2-inch pieces
2 small jalapeño chilies, seeded and chopped (about 1 tablespoon)
1 tablespoon plus 2 teaspoons chili powder
2 teaspoons ground cumin
2 cans (28 ounces, each) crushed tomatoes in puree
1 ½ cup water
1 can (15 ounces) dark red kidney beans, drained and rinsed
1 can (15 ounces) black beans, drained and rinsed
1 can (19 ounces) Cannellini beans, drained and rinsed
or 1 can (15 ounces) great northern beans, drained and rinsed
1 tablespoon red wine vinegar
sour cream
shredded mozzarella cheese (optional)
tortilla chips

In a bowl, combine ground venison, celery salt, sage, coriander and marjoram. Mix well. In a skillet over medium heat, combine venison mixture, onion, chopped peppers, green chilies, chili powder and cumin. Cook until meat is crumbled and done. In a large stock pot or in a crock pot on High, combine meat mixture, crushed tomatoes, beans and vinegar. Simmer until cooked through. Serve chili in bowls. Top with sour cream and/or mozzarella cheese. May also serve with tortilla chips. Serves 4 – 6.

I searched high and low in a nearby city (of modest size) for Cannellini beans…and couldn't find them anywhere. Where did I actually find them, of all places? At my local grocery store that serves our village of 1800 people. The only brand I've been able to find is Progresso. Look for them in the canned beans section *or* the canned soup section. If you can't find any, do what I did, use great northern beans. They worked just fine.

## Venison Stroganoff

1 pound ground venison
2/3 cup onion, chopped
1 to 1 ½ teaspoons celery salt
1/2 teaspoon salt
1/2 teaspoon minced garlic or 1 teaspoon garlic puree
1/4 teaspoon black pepper
1 can (10 ½ ounces) cream of chicken soup
1 can (4 ounces) sliced mushrooms, drained
1/2 cup milk
1 cup sour cream
2 or 3 cups cooked noodles or rice

In a deep skillet or Dutch oven over medium heat, combine ground venison, onion, celery, salt, garlic and pepper. Cook until meat is crumbled and done. Combine soup and milk in a bowl. Blend well with an egg beater or whisk. Add mushrooms. Combine with meat and mix well. When thoroughly heated, reduce heat and add sour cream. Stir until sour cream is completely blended and mixture is warm. Serve over noodles or rice. Serves 6.

## Venison Vegetable Soup

3/4 pound venison round steak, cut into 1/2-inch cubes, or about 1 pound ground venison
1/2 cup celery, chopped
1 cup onion, chopped
1 teaspoon minced garlic or 1/2 teaspoon garlic puree
2 cans (14 ounces each) diced tomatoes, undrained
2 cups frozen mixed vegetables
2 cups potatoes, peeled and cubed
1 can (4 ounces) sliced mushrooms
1 can (14 ½ ounces) beef broth
2 cups water
1 tablespoon sugar
1 teaspoon salt
1/2 cup quick cooking barley (optional)

In a skillet over medium heat, combine venison steak cubes, celery, onion and garlic. Cook until meat is brown. Cover and simmer for an additional 10 minutes. In a large stock pot, combine meat, tomatoes with juice, mixed vegetables, potatoes, mushrooms, beef broth, water, sugar and salt. Bring to a boil and simmer for at least 1 hour. Just before serving, add barley and continue simmering for 15 minutes. Let soup stand 5 minutes before serving. Serves 6 – 8.

 This recipe also works well with ground venison instead of venison steak bits.

## Mom's Goulash

1 pound ground venison
1 pound (16 ounces) shell macaroni
2 cans (28 ounces) diced tomatoes with juice
4-1/2-inch slices of processed cheese spread, diced
1/3 cup onion, diced
additional tomato juice, if desired

Boil macaroni for about 8 minutes (till not quite tender). While macaroni is boiling, Combine ground venison and onion in a Dutch oven or large stock pot over medium heat. Cook until venison is crumbled and done. Combine macaroni and tomatoes (with juice) with meat mixture. Cook until heated through. Add cheese cubes and stir until cheese is melted. Add a little bit of water or additional tomato juice, if needed. Salt to taste and serve warm. Serves 4 – 6.

## Southwest Potato Soup

1 pound venison steak, cut into cubes, or 1 pound ground venison
1/2 cup onion, chopped
1/2 cup celery, chopped
1/4 teaspoon garlic salt
1 tablespoon cooking oil
4 cups potatoes, peeled and cut into 1/2-inch cubes
3 cans (8 ounces) tomato sauce
4 cups water
1/4 cup sugar
1 ½ teaspoons salt
1/8 teaspoon pepper (optional)
1 teaspoon hot sauce

Heat oil in a skillet over medium heat. Add venison steak cubes, onion, celery and garlic. Stir and cook over medium heat until meat is brown. Cover and simmer on low for 10 minutes, stirring occasionally. In a large saucepan, combine meat, potatoes and tomato sauce. Add water, sugar, salt, pepper and hot sauce. Bring to a boil. Cover and simmer for about 1 hour or until potatoes are tender. Or, cook in a crock-pot on High or Low until potatoes and meat are tender. This soup tastes great served with corn chips. Serves 6 – 8.

 This recipe also works well with ground venison instead of venison steak bits.

## Italian Wedding Soup

1/2 pound ground venison
1/2 cup crushed Caesar or Ranch salad croutons
1/4 teaspoon Italian seasoning
1 egg, beaten
6 ½ cups canned chicken broth or about 4 cans (14 ½ ounces, each)
2 cups water
1 ½ cups onion, sliced
1 ½ cups celery, chopped
1 medium zucchini, coarsely chopped (if desired, peeled)
1 1/2 cups frozen carrots, defrosted and chopped
1/2 cup frozen chopped spinach, thawed and well drained
1/2 teaspoon garlic powder
1/4 teaspoon rosemary
1/2 tablespoon lemon juice

Combine ground venison, crouton crumbs and egg. Mix well. Form into 1-inch meatballs. Set aside. Bring chicken broth and water to a boil. Add onions, celery, zucchini, carrots, spinach, garlic powder, rosemary and lemon juice. Bring to a boil once again, if necessary. Gently add the meatballs. Reduce heat and simmer 20 to 30 minutes. Add hot water as necessary to maintain desired consistency, if necessary. Serves 8 – 10.

## South Pacific Soup

Meatballs
3/4 pound ground venison
2 tablespoons green onions and tops, sliced
1/2 teaspoon ground ginger
1 teaspoon minced garlic
1/2 teaspoon celery salt

2 teaspoons cooking oil
8 cups water
2 packages (3 ounces) beef-flavor Oriental noodles with seasoning packet
2 beef bouillon cubes
1 cup baby carrots, sliced lengthwise *or* sliced frozen carrots
1/4 teaspoon ground ginger
1/2 teaspoon minced garlic
1 pound *or* 6 cups cabbage, chopped
1 can (8 ounces), sliced water chestnuts, drained and chopped
1 cup green onions and tops, sliced
1 teaspoon sesame oil

In a bowl, combine ground venison, green onions, ginger, garlic and celery salt. Mix well. Form into about 30 1-inch balls. In a large stock pot, heat oil over medium heat. Add the meatballs and cook for about 8 to 10 minutes, turning often, or until brown on all sides. Add the water, contents of seasoning packets, bouillon cubes, carrots, chestnuts, ginger and garlic to the pot. Bring mixture to a boil over medium-high heat. Then, reduce the heat to low and simmer for 10 minutes. Add the cabbage, scallions and sesame oil. Simmer for an additional 5 minutes or until cabbage is tender. Break the noodles in half and add to the pot. Simmer for 3 more minutes or until tender. Serve immediately. Serves 6.

# Main Dish Meals and Skillet Suppers

### Salisbury Venison Patties

1 pound ground venison
1/2 cup onion, finely or coarsely chopped
1/3 cup celery, finely chopped (or use 1 teaspoon celery salt)
1 can (10 ¾ ounces) Campbell's Golden Mushroom soup
1 jar (4 ½ ounces) button mushrooms, drained
1 1/3 cup water (or one soup can full)

Form ground venison into small (2 ¼-inch dia.) patties about 1/2-inch to 5/8-inch thick. Combine onion and celery in a skillet over low/medium heat and brown the venison patties, turning them often. While browning the patties, combine soup and water in a bowl and blend well with an egg beater or whisk. Add mushrooms to soup mixture. Place browned patties in a crock pot and pour soup/mushroom mixture over patties. Cook on High setting for 4-5 hours. If you prefer, you can cook this meal in a covered baking dish at 350 degrees for approximately 1 hour. However, I prefer the crock pot method because it allows the meat a better opportunity to absorb the juices and flavors. This also makes a great tasting gravy you can pour over mash potatoes. Serves about 4 or 5.

 To keep these patties juicy, trap the steam in with a tight fitting lid while browning them.

# Spaghetti

1 pound ground venison
1/3 cup celery, finely chopped (or use 1 teaspoon celery salt)
1/2 cup onion, finely chopped
1 ½ teaspoons minced garlic (or 1 teaspoon garlic puree)
1 jar (26 ounces) CLASSICO Tomato and Basil Spaghetti Sauce (or your favorite brand)
Cooked spaghetti noodles

In a skillet over medium heat, combine ground venison, celery, onion and garlic. Cook until venison is crumbled and done. Combine meat mixture and spaghetti sauce in saucepan over medium heat. Cook until thoroughly heated. Serve over cooked spaghetti noodles. Serves 4 – 6.

 Fresh out of bottled marinara sauce? Try my Last Minute Marinara Sauce, (below).

## Last Minute Marinara Sauce

1/2 tablespoon olive or cooking oil
1 ½ teaspoons minced garlic
1/2 cup onion, chopped
1 can (29 ounces) tomato puree
1 can (14 1/2 ounces) diced tomatoes, drained (optional for chunky sauce)
1 tablespoon sugar
1/2 to 1 teaspoon Italian seasoning
1/8 teaspoon crushed red pepper

In a medium, non-stick saucepan, heat oil over medium heat. Add onion and garlic. Stir until onion is softened. Add puree, diced tomatoes (if using), sugar, Italian seasoning and red pepper. Stir and simmer for about 15 minutes to blend flavors. Makes about 3 ½ cups without diced tomatoes and 4 cups with diced tomatoes.

## Mexican Rice

1 pound ground venison
1/3 cup celery, finely chopped
1/2 cup onion, finely chopped
1 ½ teaspoons minced garlic (or 1 teaspoon garlic puree)
1 to 1 ½ teaspoons hot sauce
1 can (15 ounces) diced tomatoes with juice
4-5 slices American cheese
2-4 cups hot, cooked rice

In a skillet over medium heat, combine ground venison, celery, onion, garlic and hot sauce. Cook until venison is crumbled and done. Add diced tomatoes and cook until heated through and meat is done. Place hot cooked rice in bottom of a round or oblong casserole dish. Place cheese slices over rice and pour meat mixture over layer of cheese slices. Allow cheese to melt and serve. Serves 4 – 6.

 This recipe works well using leftover taco meat. Just adjust the other ingredients accordingly to whip up a quick leftover meal that tastes like brand new!

## Candlelight Stroganoff

1 ½ pounds round venison steak, cut into 1/2 inch strips
2 tablespoons margarine
2 cups onion, sliced and separated (about 3 small onions)
1/2 cup flour
1 ½ cups beef broth
1/2 cup burgundy cooking wine
3 tablespoons tomato paste
1/2 teaspoon thyme
1/2 teaspoon celery seed
1/4 teaspoon garlic salt
3/4 cup sour cream
hot, cooked and buttered noodles or cooked white rice (just before serving)

In a large, deep skillet, melt margarine and brown venison steak strips. Stir in onions, celery seed and garlic salt. Cook for 3 additional minutes. Remove skillet from heat. Sprinkle flour over meat and stir until well combined. Stir in beef broth, burgundy wine, tomato paste and thyme until blended and smooth. Once mixture is warm, transfer to a crock pot. Cook in crock pot on High for 2-3 hours until sauce is thickened and begins to boil. Be careful not to scorch. Add more liquid (beef broth) and reduce heat if necessary. Just before serving, stir sour cream into the sauce. Serve over hot buttered noodles or cooked white rice. Serves 6 – 8.

In times past, I use to turn my nose up at any recipe that called for wine…not because I don't like the taste of a fine wine, but because I presumed that if a recipe had wine in it, well, it was *way* too fancy for my genes. I would usually pass over these snobby wine recipes for those that called for ingredients that already existed in my cupboard. So what converted me? Well, one day as I was strolling down the vinegar and salad dressing aisle at the supermarket, I noticed the cooking wine section. I also noticed that they really didn't cost very much (about $2.50 each) so I figured I might as well try them out. Instead of venturing out to the store each time I needed a new type of wine, I chose to invest $12.50 to purchase all five different types of cooking wine, burgundy, sherry, red, white, and Chardonnay. Boy, have I had a blast ever since then (and no, it's not because I'm drinking the stuff, it's because they really do make a difference) whipping up some new (but not fancy) recipes! If you've never cooked with wine before, add cooking wine to your grocery list and see for yourself how it can enhance your next venison dish.

*For those who prefer not to use wines containing alcohol, there are alcohol-free and de-alcoholized cooking wines. However, they may cost a little more and may not be available at your average supermarket. Check with your local grocer, health food store or liquor store for Ariel brand wines from Napa Valley, California. They come highly recommended in cookbooks I've read by Graham Kerr (yep, he's a gourmet hot shot, but he's a really cool one).

## Sweet and Sour Skillet Supper

1 egg, beaten
1/4 cup milk
1/2 cup dry bread crumbs
2 tablespoons onion, finely chopped
2 teaspoons Worcestershire sauce
1/4 teaspoon garlic powder
3/4 teaspoon celery salt
1 pound ground venison
4 cups hot cooked rice

Sauce
1/2 cup packed brown sugar
2 tablespoons cornstarch
1 can (20 ounces) pineapple chunks with juice
1/3 cup vinegar
1 tablespoon soy sauce
1 can (5 ounces) sliced water chestnuts
1 ½ cup green pepper, cut into bite-size pieces

In a bowl, combine egg, milk, bread crumbs, onion, Worcestershire, garlic powder and celery salt. Add ground venison and mix well. Shape into 1 inch balls. In a skillet, brown meatballs on all sides, turning often. Remove and set aside. Remove skillet from heat. For sauce, combine brown sugar and cornstarch in the skillet. Stir in pineapple with juices, vinegar and soy sauce. Return to heat and bring to a boil, stirring constantly until sauce begins to thicken. Reduce heat to a simmer and add chestnuts, green pepper and meat balls. Cover and simmer on low for about 10 minutes, stirring often, until meat is heated through and green pepper is tender. Serve over hot cooked rice. Serves 4 – 6.

 These meatballs (sans the water chestnuts and green pepper) also make great appetizer meatballs. Just run your pineapple chunks, with the juice, through your blender or processor and cook as directed.

## Venison Parmesan

4-6 venison cube steaks
2/3 cup dried bread crumbs
3 tablespoons Parmesan and/or Romano cheese
1/2 tablespoon dried parsley
1 teaspoon dried oregano
1/4 teaspoon ground red pepper
1/4 teaspoon paprika
1-2 tablespoons cooking oil
1 egg
1 tablespoon water
1 can (14 ½ ounces) diced tomatoes with basil, garlic and oregano, undrained
1/2 teaspoon bottled, minced garlic
1/2 teaspoon dried oregano
hot cooked pasta or egg noodles, if desired

In a saucepan, combine tomatoes, garlic and 1/2 teaspoon dried oregano. Simmer and keep warm until steaks are done. Place venison cube steaks, one at a time, in between two sheets of waxed paper. Pound each steak into 1/8-inch thickness with a rolling pin. In a shallow bowl, combine bread crumbs, parsley, 1 teaspoon oregano, red pepper, and paprika until blended. Beat egg with water. Heat 1 tablespoon oil in a skillet over medium-high heat. Dredge cube steaks in egg mixture and then coat with crumb mixture. Place 2-4 cutlets in skillet and cook for 2 to 3 minutes on each side or until crisp and golden. Remove and repeat with remaining cutlets until all are done. Place cutlets on serving plate and cover with tomato sauce. Serve with hot cooked pasta and more parmesan cheese, if desired. Serves 4 – 6.

## Red Beans, Rice and Venison

3/4 pound ground venison
1/2 cup onion, chopped
1/2 teaspoon minced garlic
1/2 teaspoon celery salt
1/2 teaspoon ground cumin
1 cup water
1 cup instant (5 minute) rice
1 can (28 ounces) Bush's Bold-n-Spicy Baked Beans

In a deep skillet over medium heat, combine ground venison, onion, garlic, celery salt and cumin. Cook until venison is crumbled and browned. Add beans and water. Bring to a low boil. Stir in rice. Cover and simmer on low until rice is tender and absorbs most of the liquid (about 5 minutes). Serves 4 – 6.

## Stuffed Cabbage

1 whole head green cabbage
1/2 pound ground venison
1/2 cup onion, coarsely chopped
1 egg
1 cup quick cooking long-grain white rice, uncooked

Sauce
1/2 cup onion, diced
1 cup canned beef broth
3 cups canned tomato puree
1/2 cup lemon juice
1 cup packed brown sugar
salt and pepper to taste

Remove central core of the cabbage. Bring a large pot filled with water and 1/4 teaspoon salt to boil. Drop in the cabbage and boil until the leaves loosen and are pliable, about 10 minutes. Transfer to a colander. When they are cool enough to handle, pull of the largest leaves and set aside. You'll need about 8 to 10. To prepare filling, whip the egg and mix well with the ground venison, 1/2 cup chopped onion, rice and salt and pepper. Place about 2 to 3 heaping tablespoons of filling on each cabbage leaf. Fold in the sides and roll up. Place seam side down in a large, shallow baking dish or in a large crock pot. In a large bowl, combine 1/2 cup diced onion, broth, tomato puree, lemon juice and sugar. Mix well until sugar is mostly dissolved. Pour over cabbage rolls and cook in crock pot on High for 4 ½ to 5 ½ hours or until meat and rice are fully cooked. Or, bake in a covered, shallow baking dish at 325 degrees F for about 2 ½ hours, or until meat and rice are fully cooked. Serves 6 – 8.

## Stovetop Venison and Rice

1 pound ground venison
1 cup onion, chopped
1 cup green pepper, chopped
1 package (8 ounces) sliced, fresh mushrooms
1 teaspoon minced garlic
1/8 teaspoon black pepper
2 teaspoons Worcestershire sauce
1 can (14.5 ounces) beef broth
1 can (10 ¾ ounces) cream of mushroom soup
2 ¼ cups instant (5 minute) rice
salt to taste

In a deep skillet over medium heat, combine ground venison, onion, green pepper, mushrooms, garlic, black pepper and Worcestershire sauce. Cook until venison is crumbled and done. When meat is done, add broth, soup and rice. Mix well. Cover the skillet and bring to a simmer. Simmer on low until the rice is tender and absorbs most of the broth (about 5 minutes), stirring occasionally. Season with salt (if desired) and serve. Serves 6 – 8.

## Green Eggs and Venison

1 tablespoon cooking oil
1/2 pound ground venison
3/4 cup onion, chopped
1/2 cup frozen, chopped spinach, well drained
1/4 teaspoon celery salt
onion powder
salt
4 eggs, beaten
1/2 teaspoon hot sauce
1/2 cup Swiss cheese

Heat oil in a skillet over medium heat, add the onion and ground venison. Cook and stir until meat is crumbled and done. Add the spinach and mix well. Stir and cook for 3 minutes, then add a dash of onion powder and salt to taste. Mix the hot sauce with the eggs, then pour them over the meat mixture. Continue cooking and stirring until eggs are set. Remove from heat. Sprinkle Swiss cheese over the top. Serve when cheese has slightly melted. Serves 4.

 For a little zing, drizzle a little A1 steak sauce on these green eggs and venison before adding the Swiss cheese.

## Stir Fry Venison and Vegetables

4-6 venison cube steaks, cut into thin strips
1/2 cup water
3 tablespoons soy sauce
1 ½ teaspoons bottled, minced garlic
1/8 teaspoon black pepper
2 tablespoons oil
4 cups fresh broccoli flowerets
2 ½ cups sliced, fresh mushrooms
1 small red bell pepper, cut into thin strips
1 cup onion, coarsely chopped
1 can (8 ounces) water chestnuts, drained
2 teaspoons cornstarch
1/4 cup water
8 cups cooked rice

In a bowl, combine 1/2 cup water, soy sauce, garlic and black pepper. Add the venison steak strips and mix well. Marinate in refrigerator for 4 hours. Remove steak from marinade, reserving marinade. Heat oil in a nonstick skillet over medium-high heat until hot. Add steak and stir-fry about 3 minutes. Add broccoli, mushrooms, bell pepper, onions and chestnuts and stir-fry until vegetables are crisp-tender. Combine cornstarch, marinade and 1/4 cup water. Stir well. Add to steak mixture. Cook, stirring constantly, until mixture is thickened. Serve over rice. Serves 4 – 6.

## Marvelous Manicotti

1 pound ground venison (or less)
1/3 cup celery, finely chopped (or use 1 teaspoon celery salt)
1/2 cup onion, finely chopped
1 ½ teaspoons minced garlic cloves (or 1 teaspoon garlic puree)
1 ½ jars (26 ounces, each) of CLASSICO Tomato and Basil Sauce (or your favorite kind)
10-12 Cooked Manicotti tubes or 12-16 jumbo pasta shells
or, make your own manicotti pancake with the recipe below

<u>Filling</u>
1 ½ containers (16 ounces, each) containers ricotta cheese (about 22 ounces total)
4 ½ tablespoons grated Parmesan (I prefer Sargento or Kraft fresh grated)
3 tablespoons parsley flakes
2 eggs, beaten
1 teaspoon salt

In a deep skillet over medium heat, combine ground venison, celery, onion and garlic. Cook until venison is crumbled and done. Add pasta sauce and mix well. While boiling pasta, combine all ingredients for the ricotta filling and blend well. Preheat oven to 350 degrees F. Lightly spray glass casserole dish with non-stick spray. Stuff the manicotti or jumbo pasta shells with the filling. Place stuffed pasta in casserole dish. Pour meat sauce over stuffed manicotti. Bake, uncovered, 1/2 hour until sauce is bubbling. Serves 6 – 8.

 Don't want to open a whole jar of sauce only to use 1/2 of it? Substitute 1 ¼ cup (10 ounces) tomato puree and a dash of Italian Seasoning for the other 1/2 jar of sauce.

 Trying to figure out how you're going to *stuff* the manicotti with the ricotta mixture? I find that a cake decorator press or fluted icing bag comes in handy for *stuffing* these slippery little pasta tubes.

## Manicotti Pancakes

2 eggs, lightly beaten
3/4 cup milk
1/2 teaspoon salt
1 cup flour

Mix eggs, milk and salt. Slowly add flour and beat until smooth. Using 2 tablespoons batter for each pancake, drop onto a non-stick skillet over medium heat and spread into a 4-inch circle. Brown lightly, turn, and brown other side. Set aside and continue cooking the rest of your pancakes. When finished, spoon about 1 ½ tablespoons of filling on center of each pancake and roll up. Arrange manicotti, seam side down, in a casserole dish prepared with non-stick spray. Bake as directed in Marvelous Manicotti recipe.

## Saucy Venison over Rice

flour
2-3 tablespoons cooking oil
4-6 round or sirloin venison steaks cut into single serving pieces
1 can (14 ½ ounces) stewed tomatoes
1 envelope onion soup mix
1 cup water
1/8 teaspoon black pepper
1/3 cup celery, finely chopped
cooked rice (just before serving)

Place an ample amount of flour in a small bowl to coat venison steaks. Heat oil in a skillet over medium heat. Slowly brown steaks on each side. Remove steaks from skillet and place in a crock pot. Mix all remaining ingredients (except rice) in a separate bowl. Blend well with an egg beater or whisk. Pour sauce over meat and cook in the crock pot on LOW approximately 6-8 hours, HIGH approximately 4-6 hours or until done. Serve over cooked rice. Serves 4 – 6.

## Venison Volcano

1 pound ground venison
1 cup onion, chopped
1 cup green pepper, chopped
7 flour tortillas (10 inch)
1 jar (8 ounces) taco sauce
2 cups shredded cheddar cheese
1 can (16 ounces) refried beans
1 can (2.5 ounces) sliced ripe olives, drained
1 can (4 ounces) chopped green chilies, drained
1 cup sour cream
1 tomato, diced
2 cups shredded Monterey Jack cheese
1 can (10 ounces) enchilada sauce

In a skillet over medium heat, combine ground venison, onion and green pepper. Cook until venison is crumbled and done. Drain. Place one flour tortilla in a 12-inch round (or larger) casserole dish. Or, place it on a large baking sheet or pizza pan. Spread 1/2 taco sauce on tortilla, 1/2 meat mixture and 1/2 of cheddar cheese. On the next tortilla, spread 1/2 of refried beans, and sprinkle 1/2 of green chilies and olives. On next tortilla, spread 1/2 of sour cream and sprinkle 1/2 of tomato and Monterey Jack cheese. Repeat all three layers. Top with the last tortilla. Pour enchilada sauce all over the top tortilla, allowing it to drip along the sides. Sprinkle top with additional cheese, if desired. Bake at 350 degrees F for 45 minutes to 1 hour. Let stand about 5 to 10 minutes before cutting into serving wedges. Serves 8.

 For a smaller volcano, use 1/2 ingredients and 7-inch tortillas. Or, make two smaller volcano's using 7-inch tortillas and same measure of ingredients.

# Sandwiches and Pizzas

### Quickie Deerwich Sandwiches

1 pound ground venison
1 can (15 ½ ounces) Sloppy Joe sandwich sauce
1/3 cup celery, finely chopped (or use 1 teaspoon celery salt)
1/4 cup onion, finely chopped
hamburger buns
sliced cheese

In a skillet over medium heat, combine ground venison, onion and celery. Cook until venison is crumbled and done. If the onion and celery do not create enough moisture to keep the meat from 'scalding', add about 1 tablespoon of hot water. Drain remaining juices after meat is cooked. Add sloppy joe sauce and cook until heated through. Serve warm on a bun with slice of cheese. Serves 4 – 6.

## Italian Sandwiches

1 venison arm roast (the equivalent of a pot roast) or 1-2 round steaks
2 cups of water
1 beef bouillon cube or 1 can beef broth
1 jar (10 or 11 ½ ounces) mild Italian pepperoncinis, with juice
Italian or sub sandwich buns
shredded mozzarella cheese – optional

Combine all ingredients in a crock pot and cook on HIGH until meat is cooked through (about 6-8 hours, depending on size of roast). As the meat becomes cooked, break up the roast with a large fork. Once meat is completely cooked, remove pepperoncinis and stir the meat well. Serve on a bun with some au jus (broth) and shredded cheese. Serves 8 – 10.

## Mile High Pizza

1/2 to 3/4 pound ground venison
1/3 cup celery, finely chopped (or use 1 teaspoon celery salt)
1/2 cup onion, finely chopped
1 teaspoon minced garlic (or 1/2 teaspoon garlic puree)
1 can (15 ounces) tomato sauce
1 can (14 ½ ounces) diced tomatoes, well drained
1 teaspoon oregano
1 teaspoon parsley flakes
1/2 cup onion, sliced into rings, then sliced in half
1/2 cup green pepper, sliced into thin strips
1 cup shredded mozzarella cheese
1 cup shredded cheddar cheese
1/2 cup Parmesan cheese
1 BOBOLI Pizza Crust

In a skillet over medium heat, combine ground venison, celery, onion and garlic. Cook until venison is crumbled and done. Remove pizza crust from packaging. Spread tomato sauce over inside of crust. Sprinkle with oregano and parsley flakes. Next, sprinkle well drained tomatoes over sauce. Sprinkle desired amount of meat mixture, onion slices and green pepper slices over tomatoes. Top off with desired amount of mozzarella, cheddar and Parmesan cheeses. Preheat oven to 450 degrees. Place pizza on a baking stone (if desired) on middle rack in center of oven. Since there are so many ingredients, you will need to cook this pizza longer than the crust packaging indicates. Depending on your pizza, it could take up to 18 or 20 minutes. Just keep checking and make sure the outside crust doesn't get burnt. Serves 4 – 6.

## Texas BBQ Sandwiches

4-6 venison cube steaks, cut into thin strips
1 tablespoon cooking oil
1/2 teaspoon celery salt
1 cup green pepper, diced
2 green onions and tops, chopped
1 cup frozen whole-kernel corn
1 cup bottled hickory smoked barbecue sauce
1 can (14 ½ ounces) peeled, diced tomatoes, drained with juice reserved
4 to 6 toasted hamburger or split sandwich buns

In a large, deep skillet, heat oil over medium-high heat until hot. Add steak strips, celery salt, green pepper and onions. Reduce heat to medium and cook for about 10 minutes, or until meat is browned. Stir in the barbecue sauce, tomatoes and corn. If necessary, add a little reserved tomato juice until sauce is desired consistency. Simmer for about 5 to 10 minutes or until heated through. Serve on toasted hamburger buns or split sandwich buns. Serves 4 – 6.

## The Best Tacos in Town

1 pound ground venison
1/3 cup celery, finely chopped
1/2 cup onion, finely chopped
1 ½ teaspoons minced garlic (or 1 teaspoon garlic puree)
1 to 1 ½ teaspoons hot sauce
1 can (16 ounces) refried beans (fat free or regular), optional
Hard and/or soft taco shells
shredded lettuce
diced fresh or canned tomatoes (drained)
shredded cheddar cheese
ORTEGA taco sauce – mild (or your preferred heat level)
sour cream

In a skillet over medium heat, combine ground venison, celery, onion, garlic and hot sauce. Cook until venison is crumbled and done. Place meat in a container that will keep it warm. In a small saucepan, thoroughly heat refried beans. Place all remaining ingredients in a relish party tray or several small dishes. Call everyone to the table and let them build their taco or burrito. You can also build a taco salad using tortilla chips. Serves 4 – 6.

 Old Folks Taco - take a soft taco shell and spread some refried beans in the middle. Add some ground venison, taco sauce, lettuce, tomato, shredded cheese and sour cream. Roll it all up, tuck it in and eat!

 Kiddie Taco - a more traditional, no frills, simple mix of meat, lettuce, tomato and cheese in a hard shell taco. Serves 4 – 6.

 For a bit spicier taco, add 1/2 teaspoon chili powder (or to taste) to your simmering venison, celery, onion, garlic and hot sauce.

## Steakhouse Pitas

1/2 pound ground venison
1/2 cup onion, chopped
1/2 cup green pepper, chopped
1/2 cup sliced, fresh mushrooms, chopped
1/2 teaspoon minced garlic
1 teaspoon Worcestershire sauce
2 or 3 whole pita bread rounds, cut in half crosswise
A1 steak sauce (or your favorite brand)
2 cups shredded mozzarella or cheddar cheese
1/4 cup sliced ripe black olives

In a skillet over medium heat, combine ground venison, onion, green pepper, mushrooms, garlic and Worcestershire sauce. Cook and stir until venison is crumbled and done. Stuff meat 3/4 full into pita pocket. Pour steak sauce over meat. Fill with mozzarella cheese and top with black olives. Bake at 325 degrees F for 5 minutes or until cheese is melted. Serves 6 – 8.

 To keep the goodies from falling out of your pita pockets, stand them up in a bread pan for baking.

## Mock Gyros

1/2 cup, peeled, finely chopped cucumber
1/2 cup sour cream
1/4 cup plain, nonfat yogurt
1 teaspoon olive oil
4-6 venison cube steaks, cut into thin strips
1 teaspoon dried oregano
1/2 teaspoon dried thyme
1/4 teaspoon celery salt
1 tablespoon lemon juice
2-3 pita bread rounds, cut in half crosswise
shredded lettuce
diced tomato
sliced black olives

Combine cucumber, sour cream and yogurt. Mix well. Cover and chill while cooking venison. In a skillet over medium heat, combine venison cube steak strips and spices. Cook until browned. Drain, if necessary. Add lemon juice to steak and toss. Fill pita 1/3 full with cooked steak strips; layer with sour cream mixture and top evenly with lettuce, tomatoes and black olives. Serves 6 – 8.

## Fajitas

1 pound venison round steak cut into 1/4-inch strips
1 teaspoon celery salt
2/3 cup onion, sliced into strips
1 ½ teaspoons minced garlic (or 1 teaspoon garlic puree)
2/3 cup green peppers, sliced into strips
1 to 1 ½ teaspoons hot sauce
1 teaspoon Worcestershire sauce
1 tablespoon cooking oil
Soft taco shells
shredded lettuce
diced fresh or canned tomatoes (drained)
shredded cheddar cheese
ORTEGA taco sauce - mild
sour cream

In a skillet over medium to high heat, combine venison strips, celery, onion, garlic, green pepper, hot sauce, Worcestershire sauce and oil. Cook until meat is done. If meat seems to be a little tough, add about 2 tablespoons hot water and bring to a simmer. Let simmer covered until meat is tender (about 20 minutes). Place meat in a container that will keep it warm. Place all remaining ingredients in a relish party tray or several small dishes. Call everyone to the table and let them build their fajita. Serves 6 – 8.

 For quick-n-easy fajitas, use one pound of ground venison instead of steak strips. Combine ground venison with celery, onion, garlic, green pepper, hot sauce and Worcestershire sauce (omit the oil). Cook until meat is crumbled and done.

## Authentic Sloppy Joes

1 pound ground venison
1/2 teaspoon minced garlic
1/2 cup onion, chopped
1/2 cup celery, finely chopped
1/2 cup green pepper, chopped
1/4 cup chili sauce
1/4 cup ketchup
1 cup water
1 tablespoon Worcestershire sauce
2 tablespoons vinegar
2 teaspoons brown sugar
1 teaspoon dry mustard
1/2 teaspoon paprika
1/2 teaspoon chili powder
1 tablespoon parsley flakes
6 to 8 slices of American cheese
6 to 8 hamburger buns

In a deep skillet over medium heat, combine ground venison, garlic, onion, celery and pepper. Cook until venison is crumbled and done. Add all remaining ingredients except cheese and buns. Bring to a low boil. Simmer on low for about 30 minutes. Serve on buns with cheese. Serves 6 – 8.

## Bigfoot Sandwiches

1 pound ground venison
1/2 cup onion, chopped
1/2 teaspoon celery salt
1/2 teaspoon minced garlic
1/2 teaspoon black pepper
4 sub sandwich buns, split lengthwise
butter or margarine, softened
1 cup sour cream
2-3 tomatoes, diced
1-2 large green pepper, diced
3 cups shredded cheddar cheese

In a skillet over medium heat, combine ground venison, onion, salt, garlic and black pepper. Cook until venison is crumbled and done. Set aside to cool a bit. Butter split side of all the bread. Place on cookie sheets. Add sour cream to meat mixture and blend well. Spoon meat mixture onto bread halves. Sprinkle with tomatoes and green pepper. Top with shredded cheese. Bake at 350 degrees F for 10 to15 minutes or until cheese is melted. Makes 8 sandwiches.

 For a little variety, slice a jar of whole mushrooms into quarters and sprinkle on top with tomatoes and green pepper.

## Venison Breakfast Sausage

1 pound ground venison
1 teaspoon celery salt
1 teaspoon ground sage
1/2 teaspoon ground coriander
1/2 teaspoon dried marjoram
1/2 teaspoon black or cayenne pepper (optional for spicier sausage)

In a bowl, combine all ingredients and mix well. Form into patties of preferred size. Heat a large non-stick skillet over medium heat. Add about 1/2 teaspoon cooking oil, if desired. Cook patties, turning frequently, until meat is cooked through.

 This sausage recipe also works well for any other recipe that calls for "ground venison sausage."

## Venison Sweet Sausage

1 pound ground venison
3 teaspoons brown sugar
1 teaspoon ground coriander
1/2 teaspoon ground allspice
1/4 teaspoon salt
1/8 teaspoon black pepper

In a bowl, combine all ingredients and mix well. Form into patties or balls of preferred size, if desired. Heat a large non-stick skillet over medium heat. Cook until meat is thoroughly browned and crumbled (if not cooking patties or balls).

 This sweet and yummy sausage tastes great on pizza!

Most or all of my recipes that call for ground venison were tested with ground venison that had 20% added pork (80% lean). If your ground venison does not include pork, you may come up a little dry. The easiest way to increase moisture is to add a little water or cooking oil to your skillet as you brown or simmer your meat. Or, you can also mix your ground venison and ground pork by hand. Although my recipes have 20% added pork, to make things simple, use a 3:1 ratio. For every 3 parts ground venison, add 1 part unseasoned, ground pork sausage. For example, mix 3/4 pound ground venison with 1/4 pound unseasoned, ground pork sausage. You can either do this the old fashioned way by squishing it through your hands and fingers for several minutes; or use a manual potato masher; or mix it in a food processor. Good luck!

# Steaks

### Marinated Venison Steaks

4-8 venison steaks (tenderloins, cubed, sirloin, round, etc.)
3/4 cup soy sauce
2/3 cup vegetable oil
1/2 cup lemon juice
1/4 cup Worcestershire sauce
1/4 cup prepared mustard
1/2 cup onion, finely chopped

Place meat in a glass baking dish and set aside. Combine all other ingredients and blend well. Pour marinade over meat. Cover and refrigerate for at least two hours. Tenderloins require less marinade time than other, firmer cuts of meat. Turn and baste the meat at least once while marinating. Grill or broil the meat approximately 10-15 minutes or until steaks are cooked through. Use the remaining marinade to baste meat as you grill. Serve. This recipe makes an enormous amount of marinade. I usually make half a batch if I am grilling only 4 or 5 steaks. This also makes a great marinade for boneless chicken breasts! Serves 4 – 8.

 Plan ahead. Defrost your meat the night before and mix the marinade in the morning before you rush off to work. Or, go ahead and mix the marinade before bedtime and let it soak overnight. Although 2 hours is the minimum for many marinades, we usually enjoy the steaks better if they marinate overnight or at least 8 hours.

## Red River Roast and Gravy

4-8 venison steaks (preferably round, sirloin or cubed) cut into single serving pieces
1/2 cup brown sugar
1 can (10 ¾ ounces) condensed tomato soup
1 1/3 cup water (or one soup can full)
1/2 cup vinegar
1 tablespoon soy sauce
1 teaspoon celery seed or celery salt
1 teaspoon salt
1/2 teaspoon chili powder
1 small onion, finely chopped
flour
2-3 tablespoons cooking oil

Place an ample amount of flour in a small bowl to coat steaks. Heat oil in a skillet over medium heat. Slowly brown steaks on each side. Remove steaks from skillet and place in a crock pot or in a covered glass baking dish. In a medium bowl, combine remaining ingredients and blend well with an egg beater or whisk. Pour sauce over meat. Cook for 4-5 hours on High in a crock pot or in a covered glass baking dish at 325 degrees for about 1-½ hours. I prefer the crock pot method because the slow cooking method does a fabulous job in tenderizing these firmer cuts of meat. Be sure you don't cook it too long in the crock pot however, as this sweet sauce can scorch. This sweet, yet tangy sauce makes a terrific gravy for bread or mashed potatoes. Serves 4 – 8.

 Be sure to keep an eye on this yummy sauce, as it will easily scorch if cooked too long. You may need to reduce the heat on your crock pot after a few hours. Do expect a little bit of the sauce to caramelize and stick to your crock (due to the brown sugar) around the surface of the sauce. This easily washes off after you soak your crock in some hot and soapy water for an hour or so.

## Venison Kabobs

1 pound venison round steak cut into 1 1/4-inch cubes
1/2 cup red wine vinegar
1/4 cup honey
1/4 cup soy sauce
2 tablespoons ketchup
dash pepper
dash garlic powder
1 package cherry tomatoes or 12 tomato wedges
1 package (8 ounces) fresh whole mushrooms
1 to 2 large green or sweet red peppers, cut into large pieces
1 to 2 small zucchini, cut into large chunks
2 to 3 small onions, peeled and cut into wedges
12 to 18 bamboo skewers (6 or 8-inch)
Hot cooked rice

In a glass bowl, combine vinegar, honey, soy sauce, ketchup, pepper and garlic powder. Set aside 1/2 cup of marinade. Add venison steak cubes to bowl and mix well to coat. Cover and refrigerate at least 4 hours or overnight. Mix reserved 1/2 cup of marinade with vegetables and toss to coat well. Cover and refrigerate for at least 4 hours or overnight. After marinating meat and vegetables, drain marinade from meat and vegetables, reserving marinade. Soak bamboo skewers in water for 10 minutes. Thread meat and vegetables alternately on skewers. Brush with marinade. Grill kabobs, turning and basting often, for 15 to 20 minutes or until meat and vegetables reach desired doneness. Remove from skewers and serve over hot cooked rice, if desired. Serves 4 – 6.

# Country Fried Critters

4-5 cubed venison steaks, or 1 pound ground venison formed into thin
  patties
2 tablespoons cooking oil
1/3 cup celery, finely chopped (or use 1 teaspoon celery salt)
1/2 cup onion, chopped
flour
black pepper
1 can (10 ½ ounces) cream of mushroom soup
1 ¼ cup milk (or one soup can full)
2 tablespoons soy sauce
browning sauce
1 jar (4 ½ ounces) button mushrooms or 1 can (4 ounces) sliced mushrooms,
  drained

Heat oil in a skillet over medium/high heat. Add celery and onion. Coat
venison steaks or ground venison patties with flour. Brown steaks or patties
in skillet with the celery and onion. Sprinkle with black pepper as you turn
and brown the meat. In a separate bowl, combine soup, milk and soy sauce.
Blend well with an egg beater or whisk. Add browning sauce to mixture
until sauce is the color you prefer. Add mushrooms. Put browned meat in a
crock pot and pour soup/mushroom mixture over meat. For cubed steaks,
cook on Low setting for 6-8 hours. For patties, cook on High setting for 4-5
hours. Makes a great gravy for mashed potatoes, biscuits or bread.
Serves 4 – 6.

## Cranberry Cube Steaks

4-6 venison cube steaks
1 cup corn flakes
2 eggs
2 tablespoons soy sauce
1 tablespoon dried parsley
1/2 teaspoon garlic powder
1/4 teaspoon black pepper
2 tablespoons cooking oil

Sauce
1 can (16 ounces) whole-berry cranberry sauce
1 bottle (12 ounces) chili sauce
1/3 cup catsup
2 tablespoons packed brown sugar
1 tablespoon lemon juice
2 teaspoons dried onion flakes or instant minced onion (or 1 tablespoon minced onion)

Seal corn flakes in a bag and crush with a rolling pin. Pour corn flakes into a shallow bowl. Combine egg and soy sauce and beat well. In a small container, combine parsley, garlic powder and pepper. Mix well. Dredge venison cube steaks in egg mixture then in corn flakes. Coat both sides of steak well with corn flake crumbs. Sprinkle both sides of steak with parsley mixture. Heat oil in skillet over medium heat. Brown both sides of steaks in skillet, adding more oil as necessary. In a medium mixing bowl, combine sauce ingredients. Place browned cube steaks in a crock pot and pour mixture over steaks. Cook on Low for about 4-5 hours or on High until meat is heated through and cooked to desired tenderness. Or, place browned cube steaks in a casserole dish. Pour sauce over meat. Cover and bake at 350 degrees F for about 50 minutes or until meat is heated through and cooked to desired tenderness. Serves 4 – 6.

## Swiss Steaks

4-6 venison cube steaks
flour
celery salt
black pepper
2 tablespoons cooking oil
1 can (15 ounces) tomato sauce
1/2 cup canned beef broth
2 tablespoons Worcestershire sauce
1/2 cup onion, diced
1/2 cup green pepper, diced
1 cup sliced fresh mushrooms
hot, cooked buttered noodles

Dredge venison steaks in flour. Shake off excess. Sprinkle both sides of steaks with celery salt and black pepper, to taste. Heat oil in skillet over medium heat. Brown steaks on both sides. Combine the next 6 ingredients and mix well. Place steaks in a crock pot. Pour sauce over steaks. Cook in crock pot on Low for approximately 4-5 hours or on High until meat is heated through and cooked to desired tenderness. Or, place steaks in a casserole dish. Pour sauce over steaks. Cover and bake at 350 degrees F for 1 1/2 hours or until meat is heated through and cooked to desired tenderness. Serve over hot, buttered noodles. Serves 4 – 6.

## Sauerbraten Cube Steaks

4-6 venison cube steaks
2 teaspoons dry mustard
1 teaspoon salt
1/4 teaspoon black pepper
1/2 teaspoon ground cloves
3 tablespoons packed brown sugar
3 tablespoons red wine vinegar
2 cups dry red wine, or red cooking wine
1/4 cup canned tomato puree
1 teaspoon Worcestershire sauce
8 gingersnaps, crushed
2 small onions, thinly sliced
1 ½ teaspoons bottled, minced garlic
2 cups canned beef broth

Combine dry mustard, salt, pepper, cloves and brown sugar in large mixing bowl. Whisk in the vinegar and wine. Add the tomato puree, Worcestershire sauce, gingersnaps, onions, garlic and beef broth. Mix well. Place venison cube steaks in a shallow dish and pour mixture over steaks. Cover and refrigerate for 24 to 36 hours, turning the steaks occasionally. Place the steaks and all of the marinade in a crock pot. Cook on Low for 4-6 hours or until meat is heated through and cooked to desired tenderness. Transfer steaks to a platter. If juices are thin, transfer them to a saucepan. Crumble in a few more gingersnaps and simmer over medium-high heat until cooked to desired consistency. Pour into bowl and serve alongside the steaks.
Serves 4 – 6.

### Salisbury Cube Steaks with Onion Gravy

4-6 venison cube steaks
1-2 tablespoons cooking oil
1/2 cup dried bread crumbs
1 egg, beaten
celery salt
onion powder
1 can (10-½ ounces) condensed French onion soup, undiluted
1/4 cup ketchup
1 tablespoon Worcestershire sauce
1 teaspoon prepared mustard

Heat oil in skillet over medium heat. Dip venison cube steaks in egg and
dredge through crumbs on both sides. Lightly sprinkle each side with celery
salt and onion powder. Brown steaks on both sides. Remove steaks to a
crock pot. Combine soup, ketchup, Worcestershire sauce and mustard. Mix
well. Pour sauce over steaks. Cook on High for 3-4 hours or Low for 4-6
hours until steaks are tender and cooked through. Instead of using a crock
pot, you can cover and simmer them on the stovetop for about 20 or 30
minutes. Serve with mashed potatoes or hot cooked egg noodles.
Serves 4 – 6.

## San Francisco Cube Steaks

4-6 venison cube steaks
1 tablespoon cooking oil
1/2 cup soy sauce
1/2 cup dry sherry or beef broth
1/4 cup brown sugar
1 tablespoon plus 1 teaspoon cooking oil
1/2 teaspoon minced garlic
1/4 teaspoon crushed red pepper
2 tablespoons cornstarch
2 tablespoons cold water
warm water
hot cooked rice

Heat 1 tablespoon oil in deep, non-stick skillet over medium heat. Brown venison cube steaks about 2 minutes on each side. While steaks are browning, combine soy sauce, sherry (or broth), brown sugar, remaining cooking oil, garlic and red pepper in a separate bowl. Mix well. Pour sauce over steaks. Cover tightly and simmer on low for 8 minutes. Turn steaks, cover and simmer another 8 minutes or until steaks are cooked through and tender. Remove steaks to a bed of hot cooked rice on a platter. Combine cornstarch and cold water and mix well. Add to the remaining gravy in sauce pan and mix well. Turn up heat a little. Bring to a low boil. Stir constantly and add warm water as necessary to bring gravy to a desired consistency. Pour gravy over steaks and rice before serving. Serves 4 – 6.

 Simmer times will very according to the thickness of your cube steaks. 1/2-inch thick cube steaks were used with this recipe. Shorten the simmer time for thinner steaks. Simmer a little longer for thicker steaks.

# Appendix

## Sources for Farm Raised Venison

Ash Hill View Deer Farm
RR #2, Box 3500
Carmel, ME 04419
Phone: (207) 848-3866
email: reddeer@mint.net
Web site: http://www.mint.net/~reddeer/

Broken Arrow Ranch
P.O. Box 530
Ingram, TX 78025
Toll-Free Phone: (800) 962-4263
Phone: (830) 367-5875
Fax: (830) 367-4988

Foodcomm International
4260 El Camino Real
Palo Alto, CA 94306-4404
Toll-Free Phone: (800) 445-4622
Phone: (414) 813-1300
Fax: (414) 813-1500
email: main@foodcomm.com
Web site: http://foodcomm.com

Game Sales International
P.O. Box 7719
Loveland, CO 80537
Toll-Free Phone: (800) 729-2090
Phone: (970) 667-4090
Fax: (970) 669-9041
email: gamesale@frii.com
Web site: http://www.foodstuff.com/gsi.html

Gold Cup Farms
P.O. Box 116, 242 James Street
Clayton, NY 13624
Toll-Free Phone: (800) 752-1341
Phone: (315) 686-2480
Fax: (315) 686-4701
email: goldcup@1000islands.com
Web site: http://www.1000islands.com/goldcup/

L.F.C. – *"The most unique food stuff's on the planet"*
3246 Garfield Street
Hollywood, FL 33021
Toll-Free Phone: (888) EAT-GAME (328-4263)
Phone: (954) 964-5861
Fax: (954) 964-6148
email: eatgame@msn.com
Web site: http://www.angelfire.com/biz/eatgame/index.html

Mac Farlane Pheasant Farm
2821 S. U.S. Highway 51
Janesville, WI 53546
Toll-Free Phone: (800) 345-8348
Fax: (608) 757-7884
email: macfar@pheasant.com
Web site: http://www.pheasant.com/meats.html

Old World Venison Co.
RR 1, Box 262
Randall, MN 65475
Phone: (612) 749-2197
email: pbingham@upstel.net
Web site: http://www.upstel.net/~pbingham/venison.html

Pearl's Pantry
P.O. Box 4055
Vail, CO 81658
Toll-Free Phone: (800) 544-9714
Fax: (970) 845-7690
email: pearl@foodstuff.com
Web site: http://www.foodstuff.com

Russell Acres Farm & Produce
c/o Orchard Dell Deer Farm
1797 Alewive Road (Route 35)
Kennebunk, ME 04043
Phone: (207) 985-2435
Fax: (207) 985-9089
email: RussellAcres@mail.Vrmedia.com
Web site: http://www.vrmedia.com/russellacres/

Venison World
P.O. Box S, Hwy. 83 & Hwy. 87
Eden, TX 76837
Toll-Free Phone: (800) 460-LEAN (5326)

Fax: (915) 869-7220
email: vw@venison.com
Web site: http://www.venisonworld.com

# Recommended Venison Cookbooks

*301 Venison Recipes: The Ultimate Deer Hunter's Cookbook*, by the publishers of Deer & Deer Hunting Magazine. Krause Publications, 1992. (ISBN: 0-87341-227-3). A compilation of recipes submitted by the readers of *Deer & Deer Hunting* magazine, this cookbook appeals to a broad audience. Includes quite a variety of recipes, including ones you can use for outdoor/camp cooking. This book also offers a brief introduction to field dressing, hanging the deer, skinning, aging and butchering. Very affordable at a suggested retail of $10.95.

*The Complete Venison Cookbook: From Field to Table*, by Jim and Ann Casada. Also published by Krause Publications, 1996. (ISBN: 0-87341-416-0). Offers a wide range of recipes from simple to somewhat complicated gourmet, though I'm sure you'll find plenty of yummy ones to try. This one is definitely worth adding to your venison cookbook library. Suggested retail, $12.95.

*The Venison Cookbook*, by Eileen Clarke. Voyageur Press, Inc., 1996. (ISBN: 0-89658-331-7). Most of the recipes in this book are quite fancy, though the exquisite pictures make them look absolutely irresistible. Includes lots of beautiful photography. A loyal table hunter, this author offers the reader a vast amount of knowledge and personal experience regarding hunting and preparing venison for your palate. Excellent reading for field dressing, butchering and processing your own venison. Very detailed instructions. Hardcover suggested retail, $24.95.

*The Complete Venison Cookbook*, by Harold W. Webster, Jr. Quail Ridge Press, 1996. (ISBN: 0-937552-70-4). This is a superb cookbook! Harold brings years of family and ancestral success cooking venison to the reader. Chock full of hundreds of venison recipes, ranging from quick and easy to elegant. Harold also provides the reader with scrumptious and savory recipes for side dishes, breads, desserts, drinks and more! After reading this book, you'll not only be a better venison cook...you'll be a better cook! Suggested retail, $19.95.

*L.L. Bean Game & Fish Cookbook*, by Angus Cameron and Judith Jones. Random House Publishing, 1983. (ISBN: 0-394-51191-3). Most or all of the recipes in this book are very gourmet, including the venison section. However, they do look quite good if you are ready to enter the world of gourmet cooking and feasting. Includes an impressive chapter on cuts, butchering, aging of meat, taste, etc. Hardcover suggested retail, $25.00.

*Gray's Wild Game & Fish Cookbook*, by Rebecca Gray with Cintra Reeve. Down East Books, 1983. (ISBN: 0-89272-354-8). I appreciate this book because it offers recipes for the complete meal, including the main dish with venison, suggested side dishes, desserts and even the wine. Written with a very formal, New England voice, many of the recipes tend to be more sophisticated and less practical, so I would recommended this book for when you are ready to venture beyond the beginner phase of venison cooking. Suggested retail, $17.95.

*Eat Like a Wild Man: The Ultimate Game and Fish Cookbook*, compiled by Rebecca Gray for *Sports Afield*. Willow Creek Press, 1997. (ISBN: 1-57223-088-6). This book was published to celebrate 110 years of great *Sports Afield* recipes. Though the cover and title of the book suggest humorous anecdotes and stories, I found it to be rather formal and historical in nature. Includes lots of hunting and wild game cooking history and folklore, as well as tidbits of tips from past and present venison chefs. Offers a wide range of recipes for the intermediate to advanced level trained cook. Check it out if you like hunting, wild game and venison history or trivia and are ready to advance to the next level of cooking. Hardcover suggested retail, $25.00.

 Running out of cookbooks, recipes or ideas for venison? Visit your local library. While writing this book, I found the library to be an excellent resource for recipe research. There were rows and rows of cookbooks dedicated to specific areas of cooking, such as beef, pork, chicken, oriental, Greek, stir-fry's, soups, stews, sandwiches, salads, crock pot cookery and much more! Cooks by famous people such as Oprah Winfrey (or her chef), Richard Simmons, Suzanne Summers and Naomi Judd. It seems that just about everybody has written a cookbook these days...even me!

## Resources for Butchering and Processing Your Own Venison

*Basic Butchering of Livestock and Game*, by John J. Mettler, Jr., D.V.M. Garden Way Publishing, 1986. (ISBN: 0-88266-391-7). This handy little manual offers wonderfully detailed instructions and illustrations for field dressing and butchering livestock...including venison. The author served as an army veterinarian in WWII where he was instructed on meat inspection and butchering techniques so that he could teach people in occupied lands how to butcher hog and cattle. A nice little professional resource for butchering, this book has a suggested retail of $13.95.

*The Complete Guide to Game Care and Cookery*, by Sam and Nancy Fadala. DBI Books, Inc., 1994. (ISBN: 0-873491556). A good half of this book is dedicated to *game care*, offering lots of photos and detailed instructions. Venison care and processing is thoroughly described in the chapter titled, "Field Care for Big Game." I also found the recipes to be very practical and doable. Suggested retail, $19.95.

*The Venison Cookbook*, by Eileen Clarke. Voyageur Press, Inc., 1996. (ISBN: 0-89658-331-7). This book offers extensive, detailed and comprehensive sections on field dressing, skinning, butchering (bone-in or boned-out), trimming and wrapping. Eileen does a great job of easing any fears or intimidations you might encounter as you contemplate butchering your own 180 pound deer. By the time you are done reading her material, you might just find yourself rolling up your sleeves and going for it! Suggested retail, $24.95.

*The Finest Cuts – A Hunter's Guide to Processing Deer*, by Furious Films. For those of you who prefer to 'watch and learn' instead of 'read and learn', this instructional video details meat processing for deer and elk. Geared towards hunters who wish to do their own processing at home, this video reveals step-by-step instruction on preparation of cutting area, tools and carcass, breakdown of entire animal cut-by-cut, storage of meat and general recipes. Spokesman George Gonzales, an experienced hunter and professional meat cutter of 30 years, guides you through the ancient intricacies of preparing an animal from the hunt to the dining table. For more information or to order, write Furious Films, 859 N. Hollywood Way, Suite 118, Burbank, CA 91505 or email furiousflm@aol.com. Suggested retail, $29.95.

# World Wide Web Sites of Interest

**http://www.deer.com**
The World's Foremost Directory for Deer and Deer Hunting. Covers just about anything and everything to do with deer, deer hunting, venison cooking, hunting organizations and associations, new product features and a comprehensive bookstore.

**http://www.venison.com**
Venison Forum. Includes recipes, humor, clip art, chat groups, kids section, health topics and formal research. Also includes information about meat vendors, breeders, species, hunting, organizations and taxidermy.

**http://www.huntinfo.com**
Hunting Information Systems. An on-line guide to hunting-related services internationally. An outstanding web site created by fellow hunters to serve as an on-line guide for hunters to hunting-related services and trip planning information for hunting around the world.

**http://www.amerihunt.com**
AmeriHunt Enterprises – The Sportsman's Ultimate Web Site. Includes the latest news, hunting expeditions, wild game recipes, chat rooms, relevant political issues, Outfitter Guide Land, catalog and classifieds.

**http://www.fishing-hunting.com/hunting2.htm**
North America Fishing-Hunting. Directory Service for the Fishing and Hunting Industry. Features Outfitters and Lodges, Listing of Outfitters, Archery Information, Hunting Magazines, Hunting Supply Store, Hunting Manufacturers and hunting articles by their readers.

**http://www.us-outdoors.com**
Boasts over 750 links to outdoor-related products, services and information, with the "hunting" section providing the most information.

## http://www.buckmasters.com
Buckmasters Whitetail Magazine On-line. News, member information, hunting links, super shots, trophy gallery, humor columns and more. Also visit their site for Project Venison, *(http://www.buckmasters.com/american_deer_foundation/foundation/venison/venison.html.)*

## http://www.flash.net/~unicom/hungry/
Hunters for the Hungry. Established as a cooperative effort by members of the hunting community, the Hunters for the Hungry movement brings together hunters, sportsmen's associations, meat processors, state meat inspectors and hunger relief organizations to help feed America's hungry. In the past three years, sportsmen nationwide have donated hundreds of thousands of pounds of venison to homeless shelters, soup kitchens and food banks. Supporting the Hunters for the Hungry projects are organizations such as The NRA, Safari Club, Buckmasters and a variety of state and local organizations. These web pages are a volunteer effort to make such information available and help bring hunters together with those in need.

## http://www.nra.org/hunter-svcs/hsd.html
NRA Hunter Services. With over 2.3 million members who hunt, the NRA is the #1 hunting organization in America —offering a wide range of programs addressing all aspects of hunting including the development of youth hunter skills, advanced skills training and the conservation of our natural and wildlife resources. All Hunter Services Programs work toward the common goal of instilling and promoting the skills and ethics that will ensure the continuance of America's proud hunting heritage.

## http://www.christianbowhunters.org
Christian Bowhunters of America (CBA) is a non-profit, non-denominational, Bible-centered organization incorporated in the State of Michigan in 1984 by concerned Christian bowhunters. CBA is a ministry to the bowhunting and archery world. Seeking to exalt and serve Jesus Christ by leading lost people to Him, and encouraging Christian growth! Includes information on how to become a member, start a local chapter and opportunities to participate in CBA events.

## http://www.bowsite.com
Originally developed in 1995 to counter the animal rights groups and the massive communications network they were building on the web. Features a powerful communications network involving State and National hunting and bowhunting organizations. Usually the first site to publish anti-hunting threats, the Bowsite leverages thousands of visitors to communicate with politicians and organizations for pro-hunting causes. Also offers an impressive interactive section for hunting which personalizes The Bowsite for every registered user with news, information, links and fun features tailored to meet their specific interests.

## http://www.ohdeer.com
Dedicated to promoting the blessing enjoyment of venison and venison cookery. Also features up-to-date, practical advice, solutions and venison cookingsatire from readers like you! Find out how you can schedule an *Oh, Deer!* Cooking Class in your area. Order additional copies of *Oh, Deer!* for the clan or treat yourself to some light-hearted *Oh, Deer!* merchandise.

# Index

# Now It's Your Turn!

So you've read the book, cooked up some tried, true and tasty venison recipes from Chapter 9, and even whipped up some dandy new ones of your own using the creative processes as described in *Oh, Deer! The Venison Cookbook for Beginners*. Congratulations! You've come a long way since Chapter 1.

Now, YOU have the opportunity to share your personal experiences in cooking, creating and serving venison in the next edition of this book tentatively titled, *Oh, Deer! More Great Venison Recipes*. If you would like to submit your *Oh, Deer!* recipe for consideration in the next book, please send it along with your name, address, phone number and any personal, funny or hilarious comments to:

*Oh, Deer! Recipes*
8957 E. 2050 North Road
Oakwood, IL 61858
www.ohdeer.com

Since it has been my experience that for every great venison recipe there is usually a great story we can all learn from or laugh with, feel free to share how you came up with the recipe, what inspired the name, or perhaps where and to whom you served the dish and how they responded. Oh, and don't forget! We can also learn from your failures – especially if they will spare us all the agony of repeating the same mistakes!

If you were inspired to get involved with your local *Hunters for the Hungry* or *Sportsmen Against Hunger* programs, or already participate at some level, I would love to hear about your personal experiences with those organizations. How have you been involved? Who or what encouraged you to get involved? How did it affect your life? What would you share with others to encourage their involvement? Have you met anyone who has personally benefited from your donation and efforts? How has that affected you?

Lastly, I would love to know what you thought about the book, *Oh, Deer! The Venison Cookbook for Beginners,* especially those things you feel should be added or changed in the next edition. Your feedback is valuable, important and very much appreciated! Thanks!

---

*By submitting your recipe you are hereby granting the author and her publisher full permission to publish your recipe, your comments, your name, and the city and state of your residence in future book and periodical publications without any financial payment or royalty. Please indicate on your submission if you do not want your name, city and/or state published along with your recipe. The author regrets that she will not be able to acknowledge any submissions.

---